Praise for *Oh, the Things I Know!*

"Cheeky . . . scathing wit . . . Only a wiseguy of Franken's caliber could bring it home so hysterically."
—*The Seattle Times*

"Writing with the self-satirizing smirk that became his specialty on *Saturday Night Live*, Franken now takes on the advice-book genre . . . dispensing hilariously useless advice on things like personal health, real estate, and passive aggressively insulting your spouse by letting your appearance go to seed."   —*Publishers Weekly*

"Franken can make even Condoleeza Rice seem funny."
—*Boston Metro*

"Don't get too comfortable with Anna Quindlen, Maria Shriver, and their fellow members of the bromide brigade. Because Al Franken is here to puncture their comfy bubble with the barbed satirical insights he previously poked into the self-empowerment movement, right-wing radio hosts, and modern presidential campaigns."
—*The Portland Oregonian*

"*Oh, the Things I Know!* is the perfect self-help book, at least according to its author."   —*New York Post*

Al Franken is the author of *Rush Limbaugh Is a Big Fat Idiot*; *Why Not Me?*; *I'm Good Enough, I'm Smart Enough, and Doggone It, People Like Me!*; and *The Fountainhead* (written under the pseudonym Ayn Rand).

AL FRANKEN
Ph.D. (Hon.)

Oh, the Things I Know!

A Guide to Success, or, Failing That, Happiness

A PLUME BOOK

PLUME
Published by the Penguin Group
Penguin Putnam Inc., 375 Hudson Street, New York, New York 10014, U.S.A.
Penguin Books Ltd, 80 Strand, London WC2R 0RL, England
Penguin Books Australia Ltd, 250 Camberwell Road,
Camberwell, Victoria 3124, Australia
Penguin Books Canada Ltd, 10 Alcorn Avenue,
Toronto, Ontario, Canada M4V 3B2
Penguin Books (N.Z.) Ltd, Cnr Rosedale and Airborne Roads,
Albany, Auckland 1310, New Zealand

Penguin Books Ltd, Registered Offices:
Harmondsworth, Middlesex, England

Published by Plume, a member of Penguin Putnam Inc.
Previously published in a Dutton edition.

First Plume Printing, April 2003
5   6   7   8   9   10

Ⓟ REGISTERED TRADEMARK—MARCA REGISTRADA

The Library of Congress has catalogued the Dutton edition as follows:

Franken, Al.
Oh, the things I know! : a guide to success, or,
failing that, happiness / by Al Franken.
p.   cm.
ISBN 0-525-94673-X (hc.)
ISBN 0-452-28450-3 (pbk.)
1. Conduct of life. I. Title.
BF637.C5 F73 2002
158'.02'07—dc21   2002025535

Printed in the United States of America
Original hardcover design by Eve L. Kirch

BOOKS ARE AVAILABLE AT QUANTITY DISCOUNTS WHEN USED TO PROMOTE PROD-
UCTS OR SERVICES. FOR INFORMATION PLEASE WRITE TO PREMIUM MARKETING DI-
VISION, PENGUIN PUTNAM INC., 375 HUDSON STREET, NEW YORK, NEW YORK 10014.

For Oprah

Contents

~

Contents

BOOK TWO

CONTENTS

BOOK THREE

To the Reader

~

I've never met you. I don't know much about you. But I do know you have unlimited potential. You can do anything you really set your mind to. And be anything you really want to be—What a crock, huh?! Look, I'm not going to sugarcoat this. Your life is going to have a lot of ups and downs. Some of you who read this will have miserable lives and be disappointments to your parents, your children, your spouse, and to yourself. And to some extent, to me. Because after all, you've read this book, or at least this part of it, and still made a mess of things. But I'm not here to add to your burden. No, I'm here to lighten it—with wisdom, with humor, and with a firm belief that no one piece of advice works for everyone.

Oh, You Shouldn't Skip
the Introduction!

~

One of my biggest regrets, and I have many, is that my father never gave me any advice. Not because I wanted to hear what he had to say. (While he was a happy man, he was not what you would call successful.) It's just that if Dad had told me something clever or even useful, I could be passing it on to you right now and my job would be that much easier.

But then I thought that perhaps by not giving me any advice, he was giving me the best advice of all. Which is that there are no shortcuts, that you have to do the heavy lifting for yourself, make your own mistakes, and learn things the hard way. Thanks, Dad. Thanks a lot!

And although he never gave me advice, and I had to learn about the birds and the bees from my piano teacher, I realize now everything I know about being a good parent is based on my dad's example. It's not that I know that much about being a good parent, but I did learn one thing, which is actually the only piece of what can pass for advice that I've ever felt comfortable giving to others. It is quite simply this.

Quantity time *is* quality time. My dad never took me horseback riding. We never went white-water rafting. He never gave me the seven-thousand-dollar fully functional scale model of a Ferrari that I coveted when I was twelve. But he did spend time with me. Not necessarily quality time, but quantity time, hours and hours and hours of nonproductive, aimless quantity time.

What did we do with this quantity time? Mainly, we watched television, hours and hours and hours of television. My fondest memories of childhood are of sitting on the couch watching comedians on TV with my parents. Dad loved George Burns, Jack Benny, and Phil Silvers. But his favorite was Buddy Hackett.

Now, my dad smoked a pipe for fifty years, and by that I mean he inhaled, risking not just mouth cancer, but lung cancer, which eventually killed him at age eighty-five. Still, he loved that pipe.

When Dad got on a laughing jag, at a certain point he would begin to cough uncontrollably, loosening the phlegm in his inflamed lungs. It was never long before the phlegm made its way up his windpipe and into the handkerchief that he always carried with him for just such an eventuality. This was even more disgusting than I'm making it sound. For some reason this never bothered *me*. But every time Johnny Carson would say, "Ladies and gentlemen, please welcome Mr. Buddy Hackett," my mother would get up and leave the room.

And so it was this quantity time spent with my father, laughing and coughing up phlegm, that inspired me in choosing my life's work: making people laugh and raising money for the American Lung Association. So, no, my father never imparted a pithy aphorism or even a carefully thought out explanation of the human reproductive system. Still, he was an inspiration. And, in the spirit of the nontraditional advice I received from my father and the more professional (and effective) advice you can get from people like Oprah Winfrey, I have embarked upon this book in which I will set down the wisdom I have accumulated in fifty short years on this earth. Not just for my own two children, the eldest of whom will be graduating from college next year, but for the general public as well. Because, you see, I think of you all as my children. Let's get started.

First off, don't smoke a pipe.

======

INTRODUCTION SUMMARY

Giving advice presents unique challenges to both the advice giver and the recipient of the advice. For the advice to be effective, both must share a commitment to the advising process, an open mind as to the validity of the advice being given, and a determination to act upon the advice, if the advice does not seem crazy. Our journey has started. Good luck!

Book One

CHAPTER 1

~

Oh, the Mistakes You'll Keep Repeating!

Right off the bat, let's put to rest some misconceptions about who should and who shouldn't be writing advice books. There's no point in getting advice from hopeless failures. A hopeless failure has experience with only one mode of living, the hopeless failure mode, and can only give advice of a negative variety: "Don't do what I did." "Don't do this." "Don't do that." And no matter what hopeless failures tell you, life is much more about deciding what to do than what *not* to do.

On the other hand, enormous successes have little to offer in the way of practical advice for ordinary people. Because of their enormous success they are so far removed from the struggles faced by the rest of us that their advice tends toward matters Olympian, of interest only to other mega-successful people. For example, you probably won't be interested in how to approach the crucial decisions about the layout of your private jet cabin. I can remember wasting a day and a half reading billionaire Paul Allen's *Should the Seats Face Each Other, or All Face Forward?* (The answer, if you care, is that they should all be swivel seats, which can be locked in place for takeoff or landing.)

No. The perfect person to write an advice book is me. Someone who is *very* successful and yet still flies commercial, albeit first class, separated from ordinary people by no more than a flimsy curtain. I know what it's like to struggle, or at least have some dim recollection. As a successful person, I have to make decisions every day that put practical advice, advice that I plan to pass on to you, into action. And yet I'm not so enormously successful that I don't have time to write, or at least dictate, this book.

Some readers might think that because I am so successful, I have never made a mistake. If you're one of those, stop reading right now, because, frankly, you're hopeless. Even the most successful people make mistakes, and some have even learned from their mistakes.

Most people, for example, would consider Microsoft founder Bill Gates successful. And I guess if you equate success with wealth, power, a stable and happy home life, and a fulfilling role in society as a philanthropist and a highly esteemed thinker, then, yes, I suppose Bill

Gates is successful. But in any event, let's not argue about that here.

What most people don't realize is that Bill Gates has made lots of mistakes, many more than I have. One of Bill Gates's biggest mistakes was bundling his Microsoft Internet Explorer browser with his best-selling Windows software in a manner deemed anticompetitive and monopolistic by Judge Thomas Penfield Jackson of the United States First District Circuit. But Gates learned from his mistake, and has promised to unbundle the software to the minimum extent necessary to reach the threshold of fair competitive practice as interpreted by the current, business-friendly Bush administration.

One of the many areas in which I have succeeded is as a public speaker. In any given year, I make literally hundreds of speeches to corporate groups, trade associations, and, my favorite, colleges and universities. Right now, in fact, I am on a plane writing this book during some "downtime" en route to Spokane, Washington, where I will be giving my standard speech, "Winners Aren't Born, They're Made" to the students of Gonzaga College.

But I wasn't always in such great demand as a speaker. Particularly after a series of disastrous commencement addresses I gave in the early eighties. These were mistakes. And I learned from them.

Take for example the first commencement address I ever gave. It was at Hartford State Technical College, where I was a last-minute replacement for Undersecretary of the Navy Warren Untemeyer, who had been delayed by an unexpected indictment. Funny story. The message my housekeeper passed along led me to believe I was speaking at *Harvard*, not *Hartford* State Technical College. By the time it was straightened out and I had arrived in Hartford from New York, via Cambridge, I was so tired, disappointed, and frankly, angry at the graduates, that I'm afraid I allowed my feelings to color my judgment on what sort of speech to give. I took a very hard line with that year's class from HSTC.

I began with a quote from Goethe, whose most famous work, *The Sorrows of Young Werther,* deals with the depression and eventual suicide of an obsessive university student. Here then is my first, and second-least successful, commencement address:

> When I was first asked to speak at Hartford State Technical College, I jumped at the opportunity. Because, you see, I thought I had been asked to speak at Harvard, which would have been quite an honor. But instead I am here with you, the nation's future air conditioner repairmen. Let's try to make the best of it.
>
> Goethe once said, "A useless life is an early death."

In Goethe's terms, most of you are already dead. Because most of you will live useless lives. You will, you will, and you will. [Here I pointed for dramatic effect at several particularly useless-looking graduates and then at a man who I later learned was Dr. Jonas Salk, discoverer of the polio vaccine, who was there to receive an honorary degree and give a serious address to contrast with my supposedly humorous one.]

If Dr. Jonas Salk were here, he would tell you the key to living a useful life like his is to expect the unexpected. [And here I proceeded to tell several anecdotes about the discovery of the polio vaccine which Dr. Salk had intended to tell himself, thus expanding the scope of the disaster.]

But back to Goethe, and please remember that I prepared this speech for Harvard students, so it will probably be way over your heads.

As the booing began, I became hostile and openly combative and concluded my address, amid a flurry of catcalls and thrown objects, by giving the graduates and their families the finger.

Let's take a look at what I did wrong. First, there was my housekeeper, who was responsible for the entire debacle. She simply had to go. Second, when challenged by an unexpected situation (speaking at Hartford rather than

Harvard), I had behaved irrationally instead of trying to adapt to the new environment as Dr. Salk would have done.

But did I learn from my mistakes? Yes and no, but mainly no. A year later I was asked to speak to the graduating class of Lewis and Clark University in Portland, Oregon, where I received an honorary doctorate along with Connie Chung and Wolfgang Puck. This time my strategy was to start my speech with a bit of extremely personal information that would get the audience on my side. See if you can tell what went wrong.

Friends, family members, distinguished faculty, graduating seniors, Connie and Wolfgang. Three weeks ago I was diagnosed with pancreatic cancer. [Wolfgang's gasp could be heard over the shocked silence of the crowd.] It is a lethal and particularly painful form of the disease. I was told I had at most six months to live. Some of you probably pity me. But don't pity me. See, I pity you. Because while I have been sentenced to death, you have received a far harsher judgment. You have been sentenced to life. Without parole. You have, and you have, and you have. [And here I did the pointing thing.]

Aside from repeating the pointing mistake, what did I do wrong? Should I have just given up making commencement addresses? Or could I learn from my mistakes? Maury Povich, Connie's husband, took me aside and, after recommending an oncologist who had recently appeared on his program, gave me the key. "Al," Maury began, "personally I loved your speech. But I think you may have lost the crowd by being so negative. Remember, this is a big day for them. They want to be inspired and uplifted. Not criticized and harangued."

As I listened to Wolfgang explain to a delighted audience how life was like a pizza, I realized that Maury had a point. Why, other than having terminal cancer, was I being so damned negative? It was because I was making the biggest mistake of all. Even before I had been diagnosed, I had always been something of a pessimist. I vowed that in my last six months, give or take, I would see the glass not as half empty, but as three-quarters full.

Putting my new outlook on life into practice, it was with a hopeful attitude that I went to get a second opinion from the Oncologist to the Stars, Dr. Howard Schickler. I was immediately rewarded with a diagnosis not of cancer, but of "not cancer." And this from the man who had made his name by spotting Steve McQueen's tumor when it was no larger than the period at the end of this sentence•

I was, frankly, giddy. My death sentence had been commuted! My cancer was gone, as if it had never been there, which, I suspect, it hadn't. And to this day, when I criticize or harass a college graduation class, I am careful to soften the blow with some words of hope and encouragement. And I always end my speeches with the same words of wisdom:

"Always get a second opinion!"

———

CHAPTER SUMMARY

Mistakes are a part of being human. Appreciate your mistakes for what they are: precious life lessons that can only be learned the hard way. Unless it's a fatal mistake, which, at least, others can learn from.

What was your biggest mistake today? Take ten minutes to write a short description of the mistake and a brief analysis of why you think you made it and how it can be avoided in the future. Once a month, show your "mistake reports" to the friend or mentor you have designated as your "mistake sponsor."

CHAPTER 2

~

Oh, the Advice You Should Ignore!

A lot of advice comes in the form of quotes from famous, successful, and/or wise people. For example, in her book *A Short Guide to a Happy Life,* the novelist and columnist Anna Quindlen quotes Yogi Berra, the late Senator Paul Tsongas, John Lennon, and her father. Let's take a look at these one by one.

Anna's Yogi Berra quote: "When you come to a fork in the road, take it" belongs to a category that I call "cute, but useless," which includes, among other things, every other Yogi Berra quote. ("It ain't over till it's over," etc.) To be fair to Yogi, when he made the fork statement, if in fact he actually did, he probably never imagined that Anna Quindlen would write a book about it.

The John Lennon quote, "Life's what happens to you while you're making other plans," is under the category I call "true, but obvious." We are all guilty at one time or another of giving "true, but obvious" advice. For example, when Britney Spears recently launched her "If You Have Sex in Southern Africa, Wear a Condom" campaign with a sold-out show in Harare, Zimbabwe, she was giving true, but obvious advice.

Old Man Quindlen's quote, "If you win the rat race, you're still a rat," is in a third category I call "all-purpose excuses not to succeed." My version of that quote goes, "If you win the rat race, you will never have trouble feeding your family."

The Tsongas quote is the most interesting of the four, though not in itself worth the $12.95 suggested retail price of Anna's book: "No man on his deathbed ever said, 'I wish I'd spent more time at the office.' " While at first blush this may seem to fall into the same category as Mr. Quindlen's excuse for laziness, there's actually a bigger problem here. While I am tempted to give Tsongas a break, because like Lennon, and possibly Mr. Quindlen, he is dead, this quote falls into a category I call "quotes that are simply wrong." I am certain many people have died immediately after saying, "You know, if I had spent more time at the office in my twenties and thirties, I would have accomplished more and been much happier." And how does Tsongas know that no one ever said, for example, "I wish I had spent more time at the office and less time in prison"?

Anna Quindlen is not the only person guilty of passing along bad advice. Maria Shriver's best-seller *Ten Things I Wish I'd Known Before I Went Out into the Real World* is absolutely chockablock with some of the worst advice going. For example, the first thing she wishes she'd known before she went out into the real world is: Pinpoint your passion. You know who really pinpointed his passion? Former Enron CEO Kenneth Lay. He had a passion. A passion for business. A special kind of business. One which involved making a fortune by stealing from his employees and stockholders. There are many people who should not pursue their passion. And you might be one of them.

Although it sometimes seems like it, bad advice was not invented by Anna Quindlen and Maria Shriver. Had Americans followed Benjamin Franklin's "Neither a borrower nor a lender be," we would have been unable as a nation to build the Erie Canal, win the Spanish-American War, or bomb Hiroshima. And, of course, Franklin was merely "borrowing" from another member of the Quindlen-Shriver crew—William Shakespeare, who wrote thirty or more plays, each one replete with more bad advice than the last.

One of the trickiest forms of bad advice is seemingly good advice that contradicts other seemingly good advice. Take for example "Know your limitations" and

"Man's reach should exceed his grasp." Which is it? It can't be both, can it? No! But for years I have bounced between the frustration of having my reach exceed my grasp and the boredom of the certain knowledge of my limitations. Don't make the same mistake. When you encounter seemingly good advice that contradicts other seemingly good advice, ignore them both. "Turn the other cheek" cancels "An eye for an eye," leaving us free to render justice in accordance to whatever cockamamie principles we happen to come up with that morning.

Bad advice will be a recurring theme throughout this book. I will both cite examples of bad advice from other people and, occasionally, to keep you on your toes, give you a little bad advice myself. But the important thing to remember is that when you encounter bad advice, even from someone you respect, you should feel free to ignore it. Keep in mind, however, that advice is not the same as "laws." Those cannot be ignored because you don't like them. *That* is good advice.

═══

Chapter Summary

There are as many forms of advice as there are colors of the rainbow. Remember that good advice can come from bad people and bad advice from good people. The important thing about advice is that it is simply that. Advice.

What advice have you gotten today? And what advice have you given? Before going to bed at night, take fifteen minutes to make a list of each. At the end of a year, take a day to go through your 365 "advice lists." Does Jan consistently give good advice? Does Edwin seem to need an awful lot of advice? A year from now you'll know the answer and can act accordingly.

CHAPTER 3

~

Oh, the Personal Notes You Should Write!

Former President George H. W. Bush is famous for spending the last part of every day writing personal notes to friends, supporters, and ofttimes, to people he just met. It is estimated that over the course of his life, the former president has written more than a hundred thousand such notes, which is why his autograph is the least valuable of any former chief executive. In fact, many political analysts believe that the relationships forged by this simple act of common courtesy were the key to his ascent to the presidency. For many times, the people whom Bush wrote to sent personal notes back. Often with large checks inside.

And there are some people who say that if the elder Bush had not been such a prolific and considerate correspondent, and thereby become president, his son George W. Bush would not have in turn become president himself. I, for one, don't buy this. I think W. got there on his own smarts.

It is never too early to develop a good habit. Why not resolve that, starting the day after tomorrow (hey, make that tomorrow!), you will spend twenty minutes writing personal notes to some of the people who have been important to you? For example, an inspiring professor, your family, or Jennifer Aniston.

Better yet, take a page from Bush's book. Start off by writing people who might one day be helpful to you. The more promising of your classmates, for instance. You know them. They are the ones who paid attention in class and who make friends easily. While they still have some vague idea of who you are, drop them a line to ensure that one day if you need to call upon them for a job opportunity or a letter of reference, they will be there for you.

I know what you're thinking. "I'm a communications major. What do I know about letter writing?" Well, calm down. I'm here to help.

- -

SAMPLE PERSONAL NOTE

Dear _____,

I can't believe the (four/two) years are over. It seems like only yesterday that we were (throwing a frisbee/ playing a guitar/trying to make sense of _____'s sui- cide) in the (quad/dorm/cafeteria).

I will always remember how you paid such close at- tention in class, made friends so easily, and promised to do whatever you could to help me in the future. What a (guy/gal)!

If there's anything I can ever do for you, please don't hesitate to ask. The important thing is that we stay in touch and always remember the great times we had and the lifelong bonds of friendship and mutual obligation that we made here at _____.

Your pal for life,

Your Name

Don't be afraid to add some personal touches of your own to your personal note. Particularly if those personal touches include veiled references to embarrassing information you may have in your possession. It worked for George H. W. Bush and it will work for you!

But there's more to personal letter writing than just networking or blackmail. It is a good habit which will speed your way up life's ladder and keep you on the top rung. Just ask William Ford, Chairman and CEO of the Ford Motor Company, an enterprise founded by his great-grandfather, Henry Ford, a man who just loved writing personal notes, particularly ones of a virulently anti-Semitic nature.

Bill has inherited more than just his great-grand-father's motor company. He also inherited Henry's personal note writing habit, which has stood in him good stead during a recent crisis. Here's what happened. Ford had made a model of car called the Explorer, which had an unfortunate tendency to roll over. That car loved rolling over more than a puppy in a pile of freshly raked leaves! Coupled with a propensity for catastrophic tire blowouts, the Explorer's love of rolling over led to an extraordinary number of accidents and fatalities. It is in this context that Bill Ford's letter writing habit came in especially handy. For example, when Ford first heard that Julio Escalante's son, Julio Jr., had died in a rollover in a Ford Explorer, the first thing he did was send a personal note in to Julio Sr.—in Spanish—saying how sorry he was, along with a 10 percent discount on any Explorer manufactured in the new Ford factory in Hermocilla, Mexico, all while carefully avoiding any admission of liability. I venture to guess that that simple note may have saved the Ford Motor Company several hundred thousands of dollars *and* kept the Ford Explorer on the road for another year and a half.*

Do I write personal notes myself? It all depends what you mean by "personal" and "myself." An enormous volume of correspondence does, indeed, come out of my office, sometimes as many as seventy personal notes a day. Each one of the personal notes is handwritten on my personal stationery by either my personal assistant, Liz, or her roommate Margie who does piecework from home when Liz is swamped. Each note, however, is personally signed by either myself or my wife. Don't think I wouldn't prefer to write each and every note myself, but if I did that, I wouldn't have any time to dictate this book. The important thing is that I personally supervise the personal note writing process, because Liz is a member of Generation Y, and therefore has trouble keeping expressions like "whatever" or "as if" out of her (my) personal notes.

*This didn't really happen. William Ford sent no such letter. Happy, Dutton lawyer?

CHAPTER SUMMARY

You may not climb to the pinnacle of success like a Bill Ford or a George W. Bush. In fact, I think I can say almost for certain that you will not. But that is no excuse not to develop G.C.H., Good Correspondence Hygiene. Personal notes are the glue that binds your network of valuable contacts together. Never miss an opportunity to make a new friend or touch base with an old one by writing a personal note.

CHAPTER 4

~

Oh, Are You Going to Hate
Your First Job!

So you've written that lucky personal note and landed your first job. Congratulations! Too bad you're going to hate it.

Why? It could be any number of reasons. It could be the long hours for low wages; the work itself could be mind-numbingly repetitive and depressing; it could be a distasteful job such as telemarketing or shaving sick dogs for surgery; or the workplace itself could be any one of the three d's: dirty, dangerous, or disease-causing. But most likely the reason you'll hate your first job is that your boss is an asshole.

The reason for this sad fact is that many middle-level managers are assholes. These are the people you will meet on your way up and on your way back down. The amazing thing is that they will be in exactly the same place, still acting like assholes. The Paraguayans know this only too well. They have a saying, "If assholes could fly, there would be no sunlight." It sounds better in Paraguayan.

To prove my point, I consulted the results of the 2000 census, which is pretty accurate despite efforts by Republicans in Congress to make it less accurate. Fully 77 percent of Americans under the age of thirty claim to work for assholes. These results are colored by the fact that an equal number claim that their parents are assholes and that all their friends are assholes. Still, it seems certain that at least half of these young Americans do, in fact, work for assholes.

Asshole bosses come in as many shapes and sizes as do actual anuses. But some of the most common types of asshole bosses are: pompous and belittling bosses, insulting and abusive bosses, credit stealers, sexual harassers, foreign-born bosses of all types (particularly Iranian), and the most common type of all—stupid assholes.

This is not to say that a credit-stealing asshole boss can't also be pompous and belittling, stupid, and Iranian. That happens all the time. But for purposes of giving you advice, let's tackle these major types one by one.

The thing to remember about a **pompous and belittling boss** is that the satisfaction he derives from being pompous and belittling comes from your awareness that he has insulted you. Don't make yourself a tempting target. There's nothing that frustrates a belittling boss more than someone who refuses to appreciate how superior he is to them. Whenever he makes a sarcastic or condescending remark, simply pretend you don't understand what he's getting at and ask him to explain. He will soon move on to richer hunting grounds elsewhere.

The more aggressive **insulting and abusive boss** is a different animal altogether. The best weapon against him (or her—let's remember that female bosses can be every bit as insulting and abusive as their male counterparts) is a whispering campaign. If your boss is insulting and abusing you, he's probably insulting and abusing others. Forge an alliance with your abused coworkers and then go over his head. If you play it right, you'll be *his* insulting and abusive boss in no time.

The universally effective method for dealing with a **credit-stealing boss** is to do inferior work. While this may seem obvious, few people have the discipline to consistently make a subpar effort. Stick to your guns. Remind yourself every day that your poor performance is denying the thief the very oxygen he or she needs to thrive.

You may think that the proper response to a **sexual harassing boss** is simple: Initiate a multimillion-dollar lawsuit. Right? Wrong. The proper response is to first make a clear-eyed assessment of the situation. Ask yourself, Can I get more from a lawsuit or from actually having a sexual relationship with my boss? The answer may surprise you. According to the 2000 Census, 68 percent of all Americans who said they had sex with their boss believed that it either helped or had no effect on their subsequent career. The other 32 percent, however, believed that having had a brief sexual relationship with their boss was entirely responsible for the wreckage of their lives and the crushing of their hopes and dreams. So this is an area where it is impossible to give an answer that works for everyone.

That is in large part because the whole subject of sexual harassment is clouded in subjectivity. Take, for example, the complex relationship of Monica Lewinsky and *her* boss, Bill Clinton, which, though consensual, was controversial because of the unequal power relationship between a twenty-three-year-old unpaid intern and the Most Powerful Man in the World. But I would like to say a word here in defense of a man I consider the greatest President of the nineties.

How can I call Clinton a "great" President? Yes, he had sex with an intern. And that was wrong. But none of our Presidents have had morally spotless lives. Thomas Jefferson, universally regarded as one of our greatest Presidents, had sex with a slave. Now, I think having sex with a *slave* is even worse than having sex with an intern. It is wrong on two counts. First of all, I believe that slavery itself is wrong. In principle. And on top of that, having *sex* with a slave is even worse. What kind of message does that send to the other slaves?! Talk about creating a hostile work environment!

Say what you will about Bill Clinton and Thomas Jefferson, at least both were born in this country. The 2000 Census reveals that there are more **foreign-born bosses** than ever. These bosses come from places like Belgium, Argentina, and increasingly, Iran. They bring with them from their native lands different cultural norms. Japanese bosses, for example, insist that employees show loyalty to the company, work hard, and keep personal phone calls to a minimum. Scandinavian bosses take a surprisingly dim view of pornography downloading at the office. Save that for the home. Mediterranean-type bosses often resent an employee working a second job from the workplace. (Remember, these are simply their cultural norms. Where they come from, people often do only one paid job at a time, which possibly explains why those countries never amounted to much.) Outside of Africa you are unlikely to encounter an African boss.

So what can be done about foreign-born assholes? Should you learn their language or at least something about their culture? No. That would be lowering yourself to their level. Instead, adopt a patient and somewhat patronizing attitude as you explain to them how things are done in America. You might be surprised how a simple sentence beginning with "That may be how they do things in Reykjavík/Shanghai/Tehran, but here in America . . ." can work wonders.

Which brings us to the one type of asshole boss that you are almost certain to encounter at one time in your working life, the **stupid asshole boss**. I wish I could tell you that there is a magic bullet for dealing with this type of boss. Sadly, there is not. You simply can't wait for him/her to be fired. In my experience there is no place for a stupid asshole boss to go but up. America's corporate Mount Rushmore includes the faces of Enron's Kenneth Lay, Sunbeam's Chainsaw Al Dunlop, and this guy I met at a Sprint event named Adil Panahi from, you guessed it, Iran. But take comfort in the knowledge that you are smarter than your stupid bosses and realize that while you may not rise as high as they do, they will always need intelligent people like you working below them at the executive vice president and senior vice president level.

═══════

CHAPTER SUMMARY

Conflict in the workplace is an opportunity for personal growth. When you find yourself at odds with a superior or coworker, consider the possibility that you are at least partly to blame. Ask yourself, What could I have done differently to have avoided the situation? When you know the answer to that, you will have the tools to create a harmonious and productive work environment not just for yourself but for the stupid assholes around you.

Addendum: At the end of Chapter 1 I made a solemn vow to include not just good advice but bad advice as well. Take a half hour to re-read the previous chapter. Can you find the bad advice hidden in the chapter? Clue: Sometimes bad advice can sound very much like good advice.

CHAPTER 5

~

Oh, the Drugs You Will Take!

Let's face it. Many of you have already taken a lot of drugs. For my generation it was pot, and ludes, and acid. For the new generation it is pot, Ritalin, alcohol, Prozac, Valium, Percodan, Paxil, Xanax, coke, special K, Rohypnol, ecstasy, Zoloft, bathtub crystal meth, Claritin, steroids, Oxy-Contin, and Prilosec.

The important thing to remember is that despite the favorable reputation enjoyed by drugs, there can be problems associated with their overuse. Everybody remembers John Belushi and River Phoenix. But how many people remember that they died of overdoses of drugs? If it hadn't been for drugs, John and River would still be making us laugh, or doing whatever it was that River did.

It would be hypocritical for me to tell you not to do drugs. I, for example, am high on drugs right now.

Prescription drugs, but drugs nonetheless. I did not buy these drugs from a dealer. I got them from a guy in my building. But high on drugs or not, there is one piece of wisdom I can share with you: Take drugs responsibly.

How do you do that? First, don't take too many, and be sure to get them from someone reliable, such as your doctor or a guy in your building whom you trust. Look for signs that you might be abusing drugs, such as the loss of a job or a spouse or frequent arrests. This is how Darryl Strawberry "got the message."

If people close to you are saying things like "Please stop drinking," or "You look like the type of person who knows where I can get some good drugs," that too can be a sign that you may be developing a problem. Here's a simple test: Ask people you really trust if they think you have a problem. Tell them that they can be honest and not simply tell you what they think you want to hear, which is probably that you don't have a problem. If they then tell you that your drug or alcohol use is completely out of control, listen to them. Don't just accuse *them* of being drug addicts or having big problems of their own.

Having a drug problem is not the end of the world. Many of today's most successful people have overcome drug addiction or achieved success in between addictive episodes. Admitting that you have a problem and getting help may be the first and second steps toward reaching a point in life where you can look back on the things you did while you were high on drugs and laugh at them.

There. Savor this moment. You have just received some of the most uplifting advice that I have to offer in this entire book. How is it that I can give such consistently valid and encouraging advice? Is it because I am a naturally optimistic and supportive person? On the contrary. Anyone who knows me, from my family to my friends to my former friends, will tell you that I am not. In fact, it was not so long ago that I was plunged into a suicidal depression simply because of a financial setback. (See Chapter 15, "Oh, the Bad the Investments You'll Make!")

What pulled me out of that depression, and the many before it, was not diet or exercise or even pastoral counseling from my priest or rabbi. No. It was drugs, pure and simple. In particular, a class of psychoactive drugs called SSRI's (Serotonin Selective Re-uptake Inhibitors). You've heard of them. These are the widely prescribed pharmaceuticals endorsed by many celebrities, including Mike Wallace, Morley Safer, Ed Bradley, Leslie Stahl, Steve Kroft, and sometimes Andy Rooney.

Before taking these drugs, I was a person I call "al." Lethargic, joyless, uninterested in the world around me, irritable, and chronically sad, al would lie in bed all day, rising only occasionally, to give a speech to a corporation or trade group. Since I began taking them, I have become a different person, a person I call "AL!" AL! is the author of this book. Whenever you encounter an especially inspirational section, you can be sure it was written by AL! Occasionally, however, al may make an appearance, as in Chapters 3 and 4, when I was making the rocky transition from Zoloft to Paxil.

I can assure you that my dosage is now properly balanced and that AL! will be your guide for the rest of our journey.

CHAPTER SUMMARY

You are the architect of your own destiny. Drugs are a tool, like a hammer, which can be used to build a house or to kill a coed. It is up to you to use your drug tools wisely. Good luck.

CHAPTER 6

~

Oh, the Orgasms You'll Have!

Sex is one of the most joyous expressions of God's love for man. During sex we briefly glimpse His ecstasy at our creation.

This is of one of many ways of looking at what I consider the most sacred of our sensory pleasures. For those less spiritual, sex can be a powerful tool for two or three or four people to forge a deep bond. For still others, sex is merely a healthy form of recreation, like racquetball or bike riding or photographing animals having sex.

But regardless of how you view sex, there is unquestionably a dark side to it. The hazards of sexual relationships are many: emotional, physical, and mental. But for the purposes of this chapter, we're going to irresponsibly ignore the hazards and focus on the best part of sex: orgasms.

Orgasm is the pinnacle of sexual accomplishment. This is not to say that the pursuit of orgasms should be the end all and be all of your sexual life. Because, like life itself, the best part of sex is the journey and not the destination. Although, also like life, the most satisfying journeys are the ones in which you do eventually arrive at your destination.

Some young men arrive at their destination too early. To them I say, next time you embark on a journey, try using a desensitizing gel or ointment. This will help your partner complete *her* journey, making it far more likely that she will go on future journeys with you.

Others may not journey often enough. To them I say, "You need not always have a partner for your journey." For those of you who don't understand what I'm talking about, perhaps I should abandon the "journey" metaphor and speak in plain language. I'm talking about jerking off, which, by the way, is *the* safest form of sex, unless you do it while driving.

Speaking of safe sex, it's time for some straight talk. It is absolutely vital that you understand the precise mechanics of sex and the disease vectors concomitant with the canonical sexual methodology before you embark upon your journey. Enough said.

There are those who say that you should wait until you are married to have sex. That is fine. In theory. The fact is that postponing sex until marriage causes many people to get married too young simply because they are so desperate to have sex. Personally, I think it's a mistake to wait until marriage for sex. I did, and I regret it bitterly. (See Chapter 13 , "Oh, Just Looking at Your Spouse Will Make Your Skin Crawl!")

Youth is a time to sow your wild oats, so that you don't have to sow them in middle age and have an affair with someone who turns out to be a total nightmare. The sad truth is you will never look as good as you do right now. And as unfair as it may seem to ugly and out-of-shape people, looks have a lot to do with sexual attraction.

Scientists tell us that the higher primates evaluate potential mates purely on the basis of two criteria, youth and health, for the simple reason that younger and healthier mates stand a better chance of helping them pass along their DNA. Scientists further tell us that males have a compelling interest in having sex with as many partners as possible in order to spread their DNA as far and wide as they can. Females, on the contrary, seek to form monogamous bonds with a single partner who will protect them during their vulnerable months before and after childbirth. These are facts, and don't let any woman try to tell you otherwise.

We are not apes. We do not live in trees. Or zoos. We have intelligence, civilization, and moral and cultural norms. And yet we still act like apes. How does all of this ape-talk explain the attraction between a Michael Douglas and a Catherine Zeta-Jones? Michael, though no longer at his physical peak, is at or near his peak earning potential, which affords him unique economic power in the society we have developed to make us better than the apes. He can protect Catherine and her baby better than a young actor of unproven staying power like Leonardo DiCaprio.

In very much the same way, I am extremely attractive to women. Which is both a blessing and a curse. Let's face it, having young, attractive women in their sexual prime come on to you twenty-four hours a day is an ego boost. On the other hand, like many married men, I would never consider having an affair because I am terrified of getting caught.

Which brings me to perhaps the best, and most original, piece of advice I have to offer my married male readers. Innumerable times during the seemingly endless course of your marriage, you will consider cheating on your wife. Don't do it. Instead, you must fight your almost irresistible urge to fuck anything with more chromosomes than a chicken. The best defense is keeping your sex life with your wife at least reasonably diverting. Here comes the tip. While having sex with your wife, think about a younger, more attractive woman. Trust me, this works. Let me explain how I happened upon this idea. One day I was masturbating. As I attempted to orgasm (see, I'm still on message), I noticed that I was fantasizing about Halle Berry. And it occurred to me in a flash. Why not use the same strategy to make sex with my wife less of a chore? Sure enough, before you could say Claudia Schiffer, I was actually looking forward to my weekly sexual encounter with my wife instead of dreading it.

Funny story. While I was on location shooting the hit movie *Stuart Saves His Family* (see Chapter 37, "Oh, Define Success on Your Terms—Not Theirs!"), I was away from home for so long that I actually began fantasizing about my wife while masturbating.

Another funny story. When people ask me how I come up with my jokes, I tell them that joke as an example of the kind of rich material you can mine directly from personal experience.

═══════════

CHAPTER SUMMARY

While having boring sex with your wife, fantasize about someone else. It works.

CHAPTER 7

~

Oh, the Orgasms You'll Fake! (For the Ladies)

In our previous chapter, "Oh, the Orgasms You'll Have!" I give advice to both premature ejaculators and married men bored with their sex lives, comprehensively spanning the entire life span of the male sexual experience, leaving out Viagra, which has been done to death, and homosexual experimentation with your piano teacher, which is simply too personal.

In this chapter you will become the beneficiary of all my knowledge of female sexuality. Of course, if you have serious sexual problems, I would suggest that you turn elsewhere. Oprah, for example. When it comes to ladies' issues, Oprah is always there with a tidbit of information, a compassionate, attentive ear, or sometimes just a hug.

What I *can* tell you is that faking orgasms is not doing you or your partner any favors. I am a firm believer in total honesty regarding orgasms. You might be thinking, "Sure that's easy for you to say. You're a guy. You couldn't fake an orgasm even if you wanted to."

That's not the point. (And, by the way, I could.) According to something I read once in my dentist's office, there are two reasons women fake orgasms. The first is to get your partner off of you. By pretending to reach climax, the woman establishes a definitive conclusion to the sexual encounter.

The second is a misguided need to satisfy the male ego by making it appear that he has brought you to the throes of ecstasy when, in fact, you are mentally making a shopping list.

The third reason that I just remembered has something to do with the fact that some women have trouble reaching orgasms. There might be a fourth reason, but I was having a root canal that day and received an unusually heavy dose of an anaesthetic.

But faking orgasms is wrong. Tell us what's going on, ladies! That way we can at least make a sincere effort to meet your needs in a climate of mutual caring and openness instead of histrionic theatricality. You may believe that when faking an orgasm, you're cheating your partner. But you're not. You're cheating yourself!

CHAPTER SUMMARY

In six of the seventeen episodes of Sex and the City *dealing with faking orgasms, the faking of orgasms is treated as a laughing matter. It is not. According to the more serious and responsible HBO program* Real Sex, *faking an orgasm is the first step down a slippery slope that leads to faking multiple orgasms and possibly uterine fibroids.*

When you have a real orgasm, write a detailed description of the circumstances under which you had it. Don't simply write, "vibrator." How did you use the vibrator and for how long? The key to unlocking your orgasm potential is in there. Trust me.

CHAPTER 8

~

Oh, If You're Involved in Hardcore Bondage and Discipline, You Should Have a "Safeword"!

In the previous chapter, "Oh, the Orgasms You'll Fake!" I discussed the pernicious evil of the dishonest orgasm. If both partners share a rock-solid commitment to keeping their lovemaking fresh and original, the necessity for such desperate measures need never arise. An open-mindedness regarding experimental sexual techniques is one way that flagging interest in the sexual process can be renewed. A simple search of the Internet using words such as "wet," "farmgirl," and "Asian," will give you many unusual ideas for ways to surprise your loved one in the bedroom.

My philosophy is simple: "It's all good. Go for it." With one exception—hardcore bondage and discipline. This could be a matter of personal taste. Some people like vanilla ice cream. Other people like being mummified in duct tape and suspended upside down from a makeshift plywood pillory. Let's make a distinction here between a value judgment, (e.g., "people who engage in hardcore bondage and discipline are freaks") and non-judgmental advice culled from hospital and law enforcement records.

Before you begin a session of hardcore bondage and discipline, you and your partner(s) *must* agree on a safeword. If you intend to gag your partner or might be gagged yourself by a leather mask, a hard plastic ball, or other device, a safe *signal* can and should be substituted. And once you've agree on the word, you must respect it, even it means interrupting the flow at a key moment.

One final note. Be sure to select a safeword that does not come up normally in a bondage and discipline event. Words like "ow," "stop," and "help" should be part of the fun. On the other hand, choose a safeword that is easy to remember and pronounce, unlike "Schadenfreude."

———

CHAPTER SUMMARY

When engaging in hardcore bondage and discipline, make sure you have a safeword.

Book Two

~

In Book One we covered a lot of ground relating to the immediate postgraduate years. In Book Two we will shift our focus to family, community, and career. But first, a transitional chapter that would fit equally well into Book One or Book Two. Or for that matter, any part of life. It concerns the importance of a spiritual component to daily existence, either in the form of organized religion or an amorphous set of semicontradictory personal beliefs, such as those held by people who believe in both angels and astrology.

CHAPTER 9

~

Oh, Pick a Religion, Any Religion!

Fuzz on a baby's ear. The rhythm of the ocean's waves crashing on a rocky shore. Galaxies swirling in the vastness of the cosmos. Raindrops falling on an erect nipple. These are God's answers to the atheist or skeptic.

I am not a member of any organized religion. I am a Jew. (I first heard that joke from a Catholic, who substituted the word "Catholic" for the word "Jew.")

The point is that it doesn't really matter which religion you are. God has a thousand faces and you only need to have one of them smiling upon you. In fact, the Hopi Indians say that being smiled upon by more than one of God's faces is very confusing and can lead to alcoholism.

Look. I don't care what kind of nonsense you believe, I can tell you that religion will be a crutch which you can lean upon in times of adversity.

I came to my faith in a roundabout way. Through my writing. For example, I have absolutely no idea what I'm going to write next. Will it be another saying from the Hopis? Will it be a statement that flatly contradicts something I said earlier? Or will it be a genuinely consistent next step toward a coherent and satisfying narrative whole? I really don't know. But I'm continuing to type nonetheless as a blind leap of faith, knowing that something will eventually emerge. This is the core tenet of my religion. Keep going. Keep going. Keep going. . . .

The Hopis say that man is closest to God when he reaches out his hand to help and furthest from God when he raises his hand to strike. This may explain why the Hopis were overrun by the far more warlike Navaho, who have a different saying, which is that your neighbor's corn will not fill your belly unless you take it from him.

I could fill an entire book with these sayings. But most of them would be pretty useless. The point I'm trying to make is that faith in *something* is better than no faith at all, a lesson the Navaho learned when they were forced onto reservations by white Christians who firmly believed in forgiveness, mercy, and the principle of loving thy neighbor as thyself.

In my introduction, I promised you this book would be practical and not simply rehash the sad history of the

Native American people. With that in mind, I have prepared a list of religions, from best to worst. I suggest you cut out this list and have it in your wallet in case you have to pick a religion in a hurry in the event of an emergency or tragedy.

WORLD RELIGIONS
IN ORDER OF QUALITY

1. Judaism (Reform)

2. Judaism (Conservative)

3. Unitarianism

4. Christianity (Mainstream Protestant)

5. Islam (Muhammad Ali/Ahmad Rashad–type)

6. Buddhism, Hinduism, Confucianism, etc.

7. Christianity (Roman Catholic)

8. Judaism (Orthodox)

9. Christianity (Fundamentalist)

10. Islam (Fundamentalist)

Like all generalizations this list should serve as no more than a general guide. If, for example, you were raised in the Baha'i faith, you may be more inclined to practice the Baha'i faith as an adult instead of becoming a Reform Jew. Good for you! As long as you arrive at this decision in an open-minded, self-respecting way, and not as the result of bullying from your Baha'i parents or grandparents.

A word on tolerance. By putting Islamic fundamentalism at the bottom of my list, I am in no way encouraging intolerant or bigoted behavior toward Islamic fundamentalists, or people who are likely to be Islamic fundamentalists, such as cabbies or falafel salesmen. It is *they* who are intolerant. *That's* why they're at the bottom of the list. I said in the hardcover version of this book that I would reconsider their ranking for this edition, *if* they showed improvement. Unfortunately, I haven't seen it.

I did, however, move Roman Catholicism from #5 in the hardcover *down* to #7 here in the paperback. You see, I agree with Boston's Cardinal Law, who said that in retrospect his archdiocese hadn't put a high enough priority on protecting children. He's absolutely right. If you get a chance to check out *their* list, you'll see "Protecting Children" at #9, right below #8: "Bingo."

CHAPTER SUMMARY

Religion is like a fire extinguisher. You never know when you're going to need it. So it's best to have one handy. Whether you are dealing with a personal crisis, attempting to guide your children with a system of moral precepts, or simply trying to think of what to write next, it is faith in something bigger than yourself that will see you through.

CHAPTER 10

~

Oh, the Things You'll Keep Telling Yourself!

Time for a reality check. You're going to have some setbacks. Time for a reality check of that reality check. "Setbacks" is just a nice word for "failures."

When confronted with failure, you will undoubtably tell yourself something like "You learn more from failure than you do from success." The *next* time you fail, you will probably say to yourself again, "You learn more from failure than you do from success." By the third time you fail, you may start to think, "Why am I failing so often if I am supposedly learning so much from these failures?" Most likely, that will be just a passing thought, and you will seek solace in your old standby, "You learn more from failure than you do from success," or some version thereof, like "Failure is a better teacher than success" or "Show me a man who is a success, and I'll show you a man who has failed a dozen times."

That last one is good for your next nine failures. After which you may begin to wonder whether telling yourself this sort of thing over and over is really getting you anywhere.

Most of the things people keep telling themselves, while temporarily encouraging, are simply untrue. Take, for example, that popular adage "You learn more from failure than you do from success." Let me give you an example from my own life, which, unlike the other examples from my life in this book, is an actual true example of something that really happened to me.

In 1995, I wrote and starred in the film *Stuart Saves His Family*. It was a failure as defined by the Hollywood powers-that-be, in that it lost millions of dollars for Paramount instead of making millions of dollars for the studio. Now, I am very proud of the movie, and if I had to do it over again, I wouldn't change a thing, except perhaps whatever it was that made it a failure.

But to tell you the truth, I did learn a few things from my failure. I learned, for example, that I would probably never again have the opportunity to star in a movie, a piece of information that can officially be categorized as utterly useless, because there is no way to act upon it. I also learned that writing is not for me. I have approached every writing project since then with dread.

And it is only due to dire financial necessity that I have undertaken writing projects like this one.

On the other hand, had the movie been a huge success and won the Academy Award for Best Picture that year instead of *Braveheart* (which was, frankly, overrated), I would have been "hot" instead of "cold." All sorts of opportunities would have presented themselves. I could have been in many more movies and learned how to act better. Who knows? I might have been able to direct a movie. Perhaps one about submarines. Think of all the stuff I would have learned about submarines if I had to direct a whole movie about them.

A single success would have entitled me to make a half dozen failures. And even if I didn't learn as much from those failures as I would have from successes, I would have learned something because there would have been six of them.

Or I might have made a witty or memorable speech when I accepted my Academy Award, like Roberto Benigni. That would have been fun.

Think of all the things I could have learned from success. So be careful when you find yourself repeatedly telling yourself something encouraging that probably isn't true. Like "It's lonelier at the top." In my experience people at the top are immensely popular. Who do you think is more likely to get his phone call returned: Intel chairman Andy Grove or a homeless man?

Here's another phrase to be extremely wary of: "Every time one door closes, another door opens." Very often when one door closes, another does open. A trapdoor, leading directly to that lonely place at the bottom.

Here's a phrase that often makes people at funerals even more miserable than they already are: "God doesn't give you any more than you can handle." There's nothing worse than feeling guilty about going crazy.

But I don't mean to be entirely negative. There are pessimistic phrases that are equally untrue. For example, "Nice guys finish last." Believe me, there are plenty of unsuccessful assholes. And being a winner doesn't automatically make you a prick. Many nice guys have finished on top, like Tom Hanks and . . . Well, I'm sure there are others. Oh, yes. There's Oprah. She's very nice.

CHAPTER SUMMARY

So why do we keep telling ourselves these useless bromides and soothing falsehoods? In reality, they're a form of denial. Next time you confront a failure, ask yourself, "What really happened here? Is it possible that there is absolutely nothing to be learned from this experience?" If the answer is yes, don't waste valuable time trying to invent a lesson where none may exist. If there is something to be learned, fine. But that's no reason to be especially grateful for having had to learn it the hard way.

CHAPTER 11

~

Oh, the Politicians Who Will Disappoint You!

I was born on May 21, 1951, during the presidency of Harry Truman. The Truman administration to this day ranks highest in my estimation of the presidencies I have endured since. During the Truman administration, I, for one, was truly happy. All my needs were catered to. I was warm, I was fed regularly, and I felt deeply loved by everyone around me. No President since has managed to do all that for me. Although I did get laid for the first time during the Nixon administration, for which I am eternally grateful.

But suffice it to say that all of the ten presidents since Truman have disappointed me, some more than others. To be fair to President Bush, though, I will withhold judgment and continue to give him a chance to feed me, love me, and keep me warm the way President Truman did.

Presidents, and politicians in general, have a way of

letting you down. But that hasn't deterred me from remaining involved in the political arena as an advocate for causes and people in whom I believe, at least for the time being. So here comes some advice. When it comes to politics, get active, stay active, keep the faith, and don't give in to cynicism.

Yes, I have been burnt. The first politician I ever did a fundraiser for was the Cambodian leader Pol Pot. Years later when I saw the film *The Killing Fields,* I felt frankly betrayed. Mr. Pot had not used the money I had helped to raise to improve the lot of his people but rather to kill *a lot* of them. I have to tell you, I felt like a schmuck.

I could have given up. Instead I learned from my mistake (see Chapter 1, "Oh, the Mistakes You'll Keep Repeating!") and vowed to do some research on the people and causes to which I would be lending my name, time, and talent. A little gun-shy, it was five years before I agreed to appear at a fundraiser for a politician, Connecticut senator Lowell Weicker. I'm pleased to say that Weicker used the money I raised for vicious and negative campaign advertising and not to round up and execute Connecticut's intellectuals.

Since then politics has become more than a hobby for me. It's become a passion (what stealing is for Kenneth Lay, politics are for me). And I've been there watching attentively from the sidelines. I have seen them all, unmitigated scoundrels like Newt Gingrich, Kenneth Starr, and that she-devil Monica Lewinsky. And flawed knights errant, like Bill Clinton, Ted Kennedy, Robert Kennedy, John Kennedy, and Patrick Kennedy.

I have accepted them (Clinton and the Kennedys) and supported them, despite their weaknesses, because after all, we're all only human (see Chapter 36, "Oh, We're Only Human"), except Newt Gingrich, Ken Starr, and Monica Lewinsky, whose flaws and weaknesses I am not able to accept. The reason for my hypocrisy is simple. The Clintons, Kennedys, and Frankens of the world are on the same side. We believe in fairness, compassion, justice, and a better America for our children and grandchildren. The other side believes in those things too, but generally opposes campaign finance reform, which our side generally feels is very important.

I'm not going to waste time in this book trying to recruit you to our side by going into detail about the importance of campaign finance reform. Political philosophy has no place in a book, no matter what Plato, Thomas Paine, and Karl Marx may say. I simply ask you to ask yourself, "What do I believe?" Once you have answered that, you must find out which politicians believe as you do, or at least say they do. Read a newspaper.

Watch a news program. Call your congressman or senator repeatedly.

There's no excuse for apathy! No other country in the world enjoys our unique combination of democracy, prosperity, and respect for the rights of individuals, except for Canada, Denmark, Norway, France, the United Kingdom, Japan, Australia, and the Benelux countries. Also, Switzerland and Bahrain. And Sweden.

If you don't want to get involved, you don't deserve the privileges of American citizenship, and should move to someplace like Canada, Bahrain, or Luxembourg, where you can enjoy the privileges of something very like American citizenship without any of its responsibilities. But I, for one, love my country and its politicians. Every four years, particularly, I stand in awe of the grand machinery of our electoral process. Except in 2000, when I stood in confusion and then disgust. Still, we were able to resolve that crisis over the outcome of the presidential election without resorting to violence, something that the citizens of Zambia can't say.

AL FRANKEN

CHAPTER SUMMARY

As I write this, young Americans are fighting in defense of freedom three-fifths of the way around the world, or two-fifths, depending which way you go. We owe it to these brave men and women to recommit ourselves each day to a stronger, better, and more compassionate America. There are many ways to do this. Voting, even at the risk of jury duty, is just one of them. Lobbying for your own special interest, such as ethanol, is another. The important thing is to get involved.

CHAPTER 12

~

Oh, the Person of Your Dreams vs. the Person You Can Actually Attract!

We all spend a certain percentage of our day in a fantasy world. While we are in our fantasy world, or F.W., as I call it, we can imagine all kinds of unlikely scenarios for our lives. We may imagine that we are superstar athletes, or that we are pirates. We imagine that we can turn back the clock and take advantage of missed opportunities or undo past mistakes with the benefit of present knowledge. In F.W. everything is possible. We may be able to have sex with a Julia Roberts, Sandra Bullock, or a Heidi Klum and then discard them as soon as they become annoying. If you're a woman, you can imagine yourself as irresistible to Brad Pitt or having a threesome with Oscar winners Ben Affleck and Matt Damon. But that's not real life. That's F.W.

A healthy fantasy life is healthy. It's what separates us from serial killers, who have an unhealthy fantasy life.

But at a certain point, we must awake from our day-
dreams and deal with the world as it is, not as we would
like it to be.

Look at yourself in the mirror. Do you have the
physique of an Arnold Schwarzenegger, the intelligence
of a Condoleezza Rice, the comic genius of a Jerry Seinfeld, the classic good looks of November 2001 *Playboy*
Playmate Amber Holiday, or the warm and sympathetic
qualities of an Al Roker? Do you have all of the above
wrapped up in a perfect package like Oprah Winfrey
has? Or do you have the physique of an Al Roker, the
comic genius of a Condoleezza Rice, the classic good
looks of a Jerry Seinfeld, the intelligence of November
2001 Playboy Playmate Amber Holiday, or the warmth
of an Arnold Schwarzenegger? Perhaps you have all of
these negative qualities wrapped up in one complete
package, like Dr. Laura Schlessinger.

Let's face it, you're not anyone's idea of a catch. The
trick for finding a mate is to look for someone who is not
as bad as you but who is within the realm of realistic
possibility. I'm not telling you to compromise or lower
your standards. I'm hoping you'll come to that realiza-
tion yourself.

That's not to say that there aren't certain strategies
you can employ to make yourself more appealing to the
opposite sex. Join a gym and use it! Not only will you

look better, you'll feel better. Increase your vocabulary. You'll be surprised how attractive a voluminous (large) vocabulary can be. It worked for *New York Times* columnist William Safire, who at age seventy-seven just married November 2001 *Playboy* Playmate Amber Holiday.

Someone once said it is just as easy to fall in love with a rich person as with a poor one. Actually, that's not true. It's *easier* to fall in love with a rich person. But to get them to love you back, *that's* harder. This is not to say that you should marry for money. That road often leads to unhappiness and addiction. No. What I *am* saying is that having an actual income can expand your romantic horizons toward the more appealing end of the spectrum.

"But, Al, isn't getting a job going to make me less attractive to a potential spouse who is looking for a 'project' or for someone to 'rescue'?" Good point. But remember, the "rescue me" strategy is a gamble. Once you've committed to finding a mate in this manner, you will be limiting your sights to a partner who has a view of relationships that can charitably be described as "fucked up." In the meantime, you will be poor, desperate, and single. Sure, it's an option. But probably one to employ only as a back-up.

Let's take a step back into F.W. for a moment. In F.W. we sometimes adopt an exaggerated view of the human potential for change. We imagine that we can turn a frog into Prince Charming, instead of accepting the frog and learning to love it as it is. If there is only one thing I want you to learn from this book, it is that stuff about life being a journey and that people don't change. They don't. Nope. Never gonna happen. The person you marry will be the same person you will want to murder five, ten, or twenty years hence.

Cynical? Sure. But true? You better believe it. Ask your mom and dad (separately, of course). But I'm getting ahead of myself. My next chapter, "Oh, Just Looking at Your Spouse Will Make Your Skin Crawl!" deals with marriage. This chapter is about the chase!

Remember. The pursuit of a mate is not all calculation and compromise. It can be fun! Enjoy the chase, whether you're the fox or the hounds. But keep in mind, when the hounds catch the fox, they usually tear it to pieces.

CHAPTER SUMMARY

More lives have been ruined by the pursuit of an idealized Mr. or Mrs. Right than by settling for Mr. or Mrs. Acceptable. Go ahead. Have safe sex with lots of partners. And during the sex, think about the person you're having sex with. Sure, they may not be perfect. But is the sex fun? Does this person share some or at least one of your interests? Do they make you laugh, not just during sex, but after it? Can you share a good cry after sex? Do you have values in common? Could you imagine having unsafe sex with this person and raising a family as a result? And most importantly, if you are engaged in hardcore bondage and discipline with this person, have you agreed on a safeword? If your answer is yes to two or more of these questions, you may have found your Mr. or Mrs. Acceptable.

Make a list of the ideal qualities for your perfect mate, and have your boyfriend or girlfriend do the same. Then sit down and compare the lists. I think you'll be surprised by what happens!

CHAPTER 13
~
Oh, Just Looking at Your Spouse Will Make Your Skin Crawl!

I've been married for twenty-six years. And I honestly believe I love my wife more right now than I did on our wedding day. But I know for sure that I love her more now than I did ten years ago, when the very thought of her would make my stomach turn.

Every marriage goes through a stomach-turning phase. Anyone who tells you otherwise is either lying to you, lying to themselves, or is married to someone really fabulous. Not that my wife isn't fabulous. (She's reading this and I don't want any more trouble).

Successful, stable marriages are not the exclusive preserve of the fabulous. I once asked the most fabulous couple I know, Madonna and Guy Ritchie, how they kept things fresh despite having been married for almost seven months. "It's a job, Al," Guy told me. "We work at it every day."

"Wow! If that's their attitude," I thought, "perhaps this'll last longer than her marriage to Sean Penn." (Who remains a friend to this day, because I did not take sides. See Chapter 76, "Oh, Nobody Wins the Blame Game!")

The point is that years ago, after the meltdown, after the affairs, the private detectives, the violence—after all of that—my wife and I made an accommodation. Not a compromise, an accommodation. We realized that our children deserved a home with two parents, who at least appeared to love each other. And it wasn't long before going through the motions of appearing to love each other blossomed into actually tolerating each other. The stomach turning, the skin crawling—these became things of the past. And as we resolved to grow old together, comfortable in and comforted by our accommodation, in this fertile soil, the sturdy rosebush of our love grew. Perhaps the blossoms were not as fragrant or as colorful as the roses on Madonna's bush, but . . . There, I got "Madonna's bush" in.

A great marriage is a partnership. And every partnership involves a mutually agreed upon division of labor. For example, as I write this book, my wife is buying Christmas presents for everyone we know, taking my suit to be dry-cleaned, and cleaning up the puddle of cat vomit that I saw this morning on my way out the door.

Later—or earlier, I'm not sure when and how she does these things—she will shop for dinner, remembering to say a kind word to Carlos the doorman about his mother or father who has been sick or died. Or maybe it's Dom. Wait, it's Dom. Then, she will pay my mother's bills because I can no sooner balance a checkbook than I can take out the garbage.

And that's why our partnership works. Because Franni is good at these things. Just as I am good at writing books. But Franni could no more write a book than I could take out some garbage or help the kids write a book report for school. How did we arrive at our division of labor? Did we hire lawyers to draw up a twenty-five-page contract spelling out in detail each of our responsibilities, specifying a methodology for adding new tasks to the list, and committing us to binding arbitration in the event of intractable disputes over the terms of our agreement? Yes. That's exactly what we did. There are lawyers who specialize in this sort of thing, and believe me, they are worth every penny.

Another secret to our long and successful accommodation is a little trick we have for smoothing over the many rough patches. It's very simple but very effective. We don't go to bed angry. We stay up and fight!

Sure, this sometimes interferes with Franni's ability to

hold up her end of our bargain by doing her chores the next morning, which can lead to more anger and yet more fighting. When this happens, I take ten pages of manuscript which I keep handy in my briefcase for the purpose and wave them theatrically in her face. "Look," I say, "I have done my work for the day. Have *you*?" In this manner I win the argument, resolving the dispute. We can sleep easily that night, knowing that neither of us is angry.

The funny thing is that if she ever bothered to look at the ten pages, she'd see that they're from a book I tried to sell fifteen years ago called *Marlin Fitzwater Is a Big Fat Idiot* and realize that I spent the day dozing on the couch in my office.

As you can see, my marriage is so important to me that I am willing to lie when necessary in order to preserve the good thing we have going. As Anna Quindlen might say, "If it ain't broke, don't fix it."

But if it is broke, and you have kids, do everything you can to stay together. If social scientists have learned anything over the last five hundred years, it's that children are the ones that suffer most from divorce. Believe me, kids would rather have two parents screaming at each other than one happy parent calmly helping them with their homework. It's just the way they're wired.

So, stick it out. Stay married. When the kids leave home, you just may be surprised to discover that this stranger you're married to is about to become your best friend.

———

CHAPTER SUMMARY

Marriage . . . Madonna . . . Madonna's bush . . . fighting . . . kids . . . friends.

~

CHAPTER 14

Oh, the Violent Television Your Children Will Watch!

You'll stay together for your kids, but will they "stay together" for you? I am proud to say that I think I have two of the most "together" kids in America. This is despite the fact that my son spends hours a day playing a video game called "Grand Theft Auto III," in which the object is to pick up a prostitute in a stolen car and murder her. It's not my kind of thing. But when I was young, I listened to the Beatles, which my parents viewed with equal horror. Today, the Beatles are considered cultural icons, revered around the globe. By the time my son is my age, the same will probably be true of the wizards behind "Grand Theft Auto III."

Popular Jewish senator Joe Lieberman likes to cite a statistic which at first sounds alarming. He says that by the time a kid is eighteen years old in this country, he'll have seen over twenty-six thousand murders on television. Now, that sounds like a lot. But if you do the math, it's only six a day. So I don't know what he's got his yarmulke in a twist about. And by the way, an Afghan child will witness twenty-six thousand *actual* murders by the time he is eighteen. And I think that's a lot worse.

If you think about it, Lieberman is a bit of a whiner. For instance, he says he wants to restrict access to the Internet in schools and libraries. I personally think the Internet is a terrific learning tool. Last year my son used the Internet to do an amazing sixth-grade report on bestiality. He downloaded a lot of great visual aids, and the kids in the class just loved them. Because at that age, they're just sponges.

But Joe Lieberman and I do agree on one thing. It's important to set guidelines with kids, not just with television and the Internet, but with everything from homework to gang activity. And while it may be okay to lie to your spouse from time to time, it is emphatically not okay to lie to your kids about anything except your past drug use.

Having children is life's greatest joy. But there are some people, and maybe you are one of them, who don't like kids, and consider travel life's greatest joy. You shouldn't have kids. Don't have them.

But for the rest of you, savor the adventure of parenthood. You'll learn as much from your kids as they will learn from you. You will grow along with them. And remember, whatever you put into a kid is like an investment, from which you will reap compound interest of approximately 6.5 percent per annum.

But ask any parent. Kids are like tumors. If you're not careful, you'll find yourself spending every waking hour catering to their needs, as you would to a tumor. It's important for every parent to maintain balance in his or her life. Don't be a slave to your child. No one respects a slave—unless he's played by Morgan Freeman.

Kids need role models. That means parents with healthy interests outside child rearing. Let your children know that you and your spouse enjoy sex. Let them see you take satisfaction from your work. Tell them that you are good at your job and a very important person in your workplace, even if you are not. That is the other exception to the no-lying rule.

Children don't need to be shielded from life's harsh realities. Remember you can't soften every blow for them. Take them to funerals regularly. Particularly ones with open caskets. Or if that's not your "thang," I recommend movies and books about the Holocaust. Give them *The Diary of Anne Frank* to read. You can find it in almost any bookstore, very often next to my books, unless my books are in a separate humor section.

Children do, however, need to feel needed. Recently, in our home, my wife handed over several of her responsibilities, including unloading the dishwasher and taking out the garbage, to our son. It's done wonders for his self-esteem. With the newfound confidence he won from taking out the garbage, he recently got up the nerve to ask a cute girl from school out to a violent movie.

Inevitably, your children will grow up to leave home and go to college, technical school, or the armed services. Does this mean your parenting days are over? Yes. Your children will still rely on you for guidance. Don't give it. They're on their own now.

Those of you who received this book as a graduation gift are most likely feeling a great deal of gratitude for your parents' sacrifice. Show your parents you love them by having a clearly defined career goal that they can easily explain to their friends. Do your parents a favor. Don't become a reflexologist. Not only is it hard to explain, but once people figure out that it's basically just foot massage, your parents' friends will be unimpressed.

As life goes on, a role reversal begins to take place. The parents become the children, and the children, the parents. It won't be long before you're changing *their* diapers as they once changed yours. Relish it!

Chapter Summary

Parenting is the hardest job you will ever love. The key to successful parenting is consistency, which I forgot to include in the chapter proper, but am glad I have the opportunity to put in the summary. Oh, and another thing. You and your spouse have to present a united front. Resolve any differences in philosophy away from the children. If, for example, one parent is prejudiced against certain minorities, you will have to decide as a couple whether to both tell racist jokes in front of them or to avoid racist jokes altogether. And remember, there are no right answers.

CHAPTER 15
~

Oh, the Bad Investments You'll Make (and the Good Ones You Won't)!

My old friend and mentor Babe Paley once said to me, "Al, you can't be too rich or too thin." This was before she began to suffer the chronic wasting that was symptomatic of the ovarian cancer that eventually killed her. (It is not true, by the way, that her husband, CBS founder Bill Paley, said, "You can't be too rich or too unfaithful.")

The point Babe was trying to make was a good one. No one likes a fat poor person. That said, money must be regarded as a means and not an end in itself. In my case, I made the mistake of using money purely as a means to make more money and wound up with no money. Hence, this hurried book.

Like many Enron shareholders, I couldn't have been more excited when the stock climbed from $45, where I bought it, to $67, where I bought some more, to $73,

78

where I cashed in my Keogh plan to put everything I had into the company, to $79, where I took out a second mortgage to buy more Enron stock, to $86, where I successfully persuaded my brother and his family, my parents, and my in-laws to invest their life savings in Enron quickly before it became overpriced. By the time the stock hit its all-time high at $90.75, I was a millionaire. I had taken a mere eight hundred thousand dollars and turned it into a small fortune, $1.1 million.

We were rich! I celebrated by buying my wife a two-hundred-thousand-dollar emerald, which fortunately she made me take back. In fact, I was at the jeweler's returning the emerald and looking at a more moderately priced ruby tennis bracelet when I received a phone call. "Al, it's Kenneth Lay over at Enron," the chairman said in an urgent whisper. "Don't believe what you hear about the stock."

"I haven't heard anything about the stock, Ken. What shouldn't I believe that I haven't heard?"

"It's just that it's down a little today," he replied. "Hang in there."

"Oh, okay," I said, thinking that maybe I shouldn't buy the tennis bracelet. "Let me ask you a question, Ken. Are you selling *your* stock?"

"Hell no," said Lay. "If anything, I'm buying more."

"Would you like to buy mine?" I asked. But the line was dead.

You know the rest. A week later the stock was trading at somewhere between a dime and a quarter. Like thousands of Enron shareholders, many of them company employees, I was wiped out. Kenneth Lay, or as my children call him, Kenneth "Lie," had actually been selling off his stock, and wound up with $150 million, enough to buy a whole emerald mine.

But in a way, this was all a blessing in disguise—admittedly, a very good disguise, like they used to use in *Mission: Impossible*. You see, like most authors I am writing this book because I am in desperate need of money. But unlike most authors, I'm telling you that. Remember the blind British poet John Milton, who wrote *Paradise Lost*? He didn't write that book because he was "inspired." He wrote it because he was wiped out in the Dutch tulip craze of the 1630s. It was ever thus, and ever will be.

So you are the beneficiary. Both from the sheer pleasure you'll get from reading of my misfortune *and* from the lessons I've garnered from the same misfortune.

Lesson One—Be extremely careful with your money. If an investment sounds too good to be true, Kenneth Lay is probably involved.

Lesson Two—Don't get greedy. Greed works for some people (Kenneth Lay), but not for everyone (Al Franken).

Lesson Three—Diversify your portfolio. Don't put all your eggs in one basket. So you've purchased stock in an Internet portal. Fine. Now invest in an old-fashioned bricks-and-mortar company, like Bricks-andMortar.com.

Lesson Four—Buy gold. In an uncertain world, precious metals retain their value.

Lesson Five—Invest for the long term. After choosing a low-risk investment vehicle like a stock index fund or a rare emerald, do yourself a favor. Don't even consider touching your investment for five years. Don't even look at it. The consensus among financial experts is that looking at it is bad luck.

Lesson Six—And this is a biggie. Follow your gut! If you find yourself using a product, invest in it. You see, I wasn't using Enron, but I was using Bounty towels. Had I made an equivalent investment in Bounty's manufacturer, Procter & Gamble, I would have reaped a disappointing, but respectable, 3 percent return rather than suffering a 99.8 percent loss.

Although money can't buy happiness, it can buy certain pills that will make you happy. And financial security, while no guarantee of outright happiness, can at least eliminate the many kinds of unhappiness that come from being financially *in*secure.

Money issues are a flashpoint in many relationships. But remember, a conversation about money is often a conversation about something else. When your spouse asks, "Can I have some money?" what he or she may really be asking is "Do you love me?" Similarly, some disputes that, at first blush, seem to be about something else, may actually be about money. When your spouse says, "Gee, I wish we didn't have such a shitty car" or "Gee, I wish we didn't live in such a shitty neighborhood," what he or she (probably she) may really be saying is: "I wish you made more money, so that we could afford a better car and a better house in a better neighborhood."

Like so many issues that cause suffering between couples (sex, child rearing, professional sports team loyalties), money matters are best resolved through a frank and honest discussion. Plan a family meeting every month to go over your books just as though you were a corporation. Are you spending too much? If so, where can you cut back? Is there anything handy you could pawn? How about that figurine your mother-in-law gave you? No? Well, what about your fucking golf clubs, then? As you can see, not only will you be having a highly productive financial discussion, but you will teaching your kids valuable lessons about responsible behavior.

CHAPTER SUMMARY

Death comes to all men, rich and poor alike, but that is small consolation to those who must die in a veterans hospital because they have no money.

CHAPTER 16
~

Oh, You Should Go to Canada and See the Northern Lights Before You Die!

Career and family are only a part of the gorgeous mosaic that is you. A full life should include a rich tapestry of diverse experiences. I could simply tell you what experiences you should have and in what order, but that would be cheating. Cheating me and, more importantly, cheating you. Yes, certain ones are obvious. Before you die, you should learn to play a musical instrument, even if it's the tambourine. Everyone, *everyone*, should visit Paris. And before you die, you should definitely have the enriching experience of making out a will.

Other life-defining experiences are perhaps less obvious. Everyone should spend one afternoon a week fingerpainting. Everyone should visit London. At least once in your life, do something illegal. And if you get arrested, remember Martin Luther King, Nelson Mandela, and Tim Allen all spent time in prison.

But if you can do only one of the many things you should do once in your life, go to Canada to see the Northern Lights! It's something that you'll never forget, and I'm not just telling you that because I'm being paid ten thousand dollars (American) by the Canadian Tourist Board to say so.

Canada is a vast country. A land of pristine forests and snowy vistas. There are long, wide beaches, huge inland lakes, and seemingly endless prairies. In short, there is something for everyone in Canada.

But Canada is more than just a land of spectacular scenery. It is home to some of the friendliest people on earth. Whether they are of French or English descent, part of Canada's thriving native population, or one of Canada's more recent arrivals, like suspected Millennium bomber Ahmed Ressam, they will always have a warm word of welcome.

What many people don't realize about Canada is that it is also a nation of sophisticated cities with all the modern conveniences. There's the hustle and bustle of Toronto, Canada's largest city. There's also the hustle and bustle of Montreal with its cultural riches. In Quebec City, you'll be greeted in the French manner with a surly *"bonjour"* or *"bonsoir,"* depending on what time you arrive. The capital, Ottawa, is the place to go if you're interested in catching a glimpse of one of

Canada's superstar politicians, such as Prime Minister Jean Chrétien or Governor-General Adrienne Clarkson.

While not a city, Niagara Falls, which straddles the border between the U.S. and Canada, is one of the world's great natural wonders. And the Canadian side is a pleasant and extremely safe place to spend your honeymoon.

Speaking of natural phenomena, before you die, you absolutely must go to Canada to view the Northern Lights. If you think you've seen a light show in a disco, wait till you see nature's light show glowing high in the ionosphere miles above you on a crisp winter night! Greens, reds, blues, purples . . . these are but a few of the colors you will see as subatomic particles streaming from the sun in the solar wind collide with wisps of gas in the outer atmosphere, releasing energy and exploding with breathtaking colors, including orange and magenta! Mere words cannot do justice, but the Canucks are paying me cash money, so here's a try: It's as if George Lucas and Steven Spielberg had collaborated with God on a drive-in movie in the sky!

Many hotels in Canada have special Northern Lights getaway packages, which may include discounted rooms, free breakfast, and transportation to prime viewing sites. To find out more call 1-800-OhCanada or visit the Canadian Tourist Board's special Northern Lights website at BeforeYouDie.com.

To make sure you do not die *while* viewing the Northern Lights, be sure to dress warmly with multiple layers. Also, be on the lookout for bears. Canada is home to many species of bears, but unlike the friendly cartoon Yogi Bear, these bears are vicious wild animals. A bear attack can ruin a carefully planned vacation.

═══════

Chapter Summary

Make a list of the things you want to do before you die. And don't wait till you're almost dead to do it. Do you want to go to China? Put it on the list. Perhaps you want to make the perfect soufflé. Put that on the list. Perhaps you'd like to have sex with George Clooney or Halle Berry. Well, sure, put it on the list. It's just a list. But, remember, anybody with a valid passport can visit Canada. And keep in mind, if you're going in the middle of winter, ideal viewing months for the Northern Lights, hotels can fill up early. Be sure to make a reservation. Or as they say in Quebec, a réservation!

ADVERTISEMENT

CHAPTER 17

~

Oh, The Weight You Will Gain!

If you are an American, chances are you are over-weight. This is true whether you're a nurse, a truck driver, or just a kid spending the summer at fat camp. I should talk. Unless I lose thirty pounds by the time I'm on television promoting this book, you will discover that I too am an overweight American.

So, what's wrong with being fat? What's wrong with an extra twenty, thirty, or seventy-five pounds? Well, that depends entirely on whether or not you're trying to attract members of the opposite sex who are not chubby-chasers.

Throughout this book I have endeavored to explain to you the scientific underpinnings for my advice. The reason that some men may be attracted to fat women and some women to fat men is that fat is in some cul-tures, for example the indigenous people of Tonga, an indication of prosperity. The king of Tonga, King Tamala-kahumdamakalamakahanee, is currently the world's fat-test monarch. For him his rolls of fat are not repulsive and freakish, they are indicators of his status as the fat-test, and therefore most prosperous, of all Tongans. If my old friend Rush Limbaugh were to move to Tonga, he would immediately be afforded the very same ele-vated status he currently enjoys here in the United States.

But here in America, the correspondence between fat and status is reversed. You remember another old friend, my mentor Babe Paley who made that crack about not being able to be too rich or too thin. Or maybe it was the Duchess of Windsor. I can't remember, we were all so drunk at the time. At any rate, in America, the further down you are on the social status ladder, the fatter you tend to be.

That's why if you want to be a winner, you've got to look like a winner. And that means starving yourself to the point of bone loss.

Don't let anyone tell you otherwise. The secrets to maintaining a healthy weight are three: diet, exercise, and methamphetamines. Of these three, one—diet—is not addictive. That's why I always advise people to start their weight loss with diet before trying something po-tentially dangerous like methamphetamines or exercise.

Do you really need that pork chop? No. Especially since you didn't even order it, and it's on the plate of the person next to you. Resist the urge to take food off the plates of other people in restaurants. Or, if you must, at least ask "Are you going to finish that?" (See Chapter 32, "Oh, Courtesy Is Not Just for Athletes!")

Although I have been asked too many times, I have never written a diet book. Frankly, I have never seen the need. There are hundreds of excellent diet books on the shelves of your local bookstore. Any one of which could start you down the path of healthy nonsustainable weight loss, followed by weight gain, followed by purchase of another diet book. It's a cycle that works for millions of Americans. But is it for you?

To determine if you are a candidate for nonsustainable (or "temporary") weight loss, ask yourself these questions: Have I ever been able to stick to anything in my entire goddamned life? Do I like to exercise? Am I Tongan? If the answer is no to all three, you may be a candidate for nonsustainable weight loss.

Temporary weight loss has several advantages over permanent weight loss, the primary one being that it is something you might actually be able to accomplish. Another fun aspect of nonsustainable weight loss is timing your weight loss to coincide with important events such as your wedding, a college reunion, or posing nude for *Playboy*.

Like everything else in life, as you get older, achieving even temporary weight loss becomes more difficult. For each year you age you can expect to put on from one to twenty pounds, until eventually you die and are fork-lifted out of your house.

The fatal mathematics of age and obesity are further exacerbated by marriage. Simply put, once married you will no longer give a shit about how you look. What's more, personal appearance can be a handy arena in which to punish your spouse passive aggressively by allowing your own appearance to deteriorate.

But hear me and hear me well. While becoming mor-bidly obese is an easy way to insult your spouse, it also exacts a toll on you. There are many other ways to make yourself unattractive besides weight gain. As I like to say, "Don't eat muttonchops, grow them! (Or one)."

Time for another reality check. Some readers may feel that I'm setting my sights too low in evaluating their capacity for constructive change. Far from it. Like the United States Army, I want you to be all that you can be. But I part company with the Army in my capacity to make you run an obstacle course or undertake a twenty-mile forced march with a forty-pound pack through an especially hot and humid part of South Carolina. Or even to eat a balanced diet designed by the Army's highest ranking woman, Colonel Louise Jamanski, head of the Joint Military Nutrition Command.

My goal in this book is to avoid magical thinking of the sort offered by my colleagues in the advice game. Yes, I might sell more books if I made outlandish promises such as those in the book *Eat Healthy, Feel Better,* but I would rather tell the truth, unpleasant though it may be, and sell fewer books, than lie to you about your potential like other self-help writers, such as the Dalai Lama.

CHAPTER SUMMARY

Hollywood is especially guilty of promoting an unrealistic body image that can be extremely damaging, particularly to young women. That would have been a worthwhile topic to get into in the preceding chapter.

CHAPTER *18*

~

Oh, The Houses You Will Covet and The Homeowners You'll Envy!

Against my better judgment every week I flip to the back of the Sunday *New York Times Magazine*, to a section called "Luxury Homes and Estates." This consists of ads for houses in the two- to eighty-million-dollar range. Would I like to own a ten-bedroom recently renovated center-hall colonial on eighty acres in the heart of Bedford horse country? Does it have a pool, tennis court, pond with waterfall, and a guest house where my friends and relatives could come to stay? Now I want it even more. Or would I rather have my own island in the Bahamas? With an airstrip and a water filtration plant? Yes, that sounds good, too. Or what about a hundred-thousand-acre ranch in the Grand Tetons? I suppose I could get used to that. After all, thirty thousand acres of the ranch are close to good schools. So it wouldn't be a problem for the kids.

These ads are what my psychiatrist calls a "suffering invitation." They tempt me with things I cannot possibly have and cause me pain when I realize I cannot have them. And, because they seem so far out of reach, instead of motivating me to buy a house, say in the town of Bedford with a kitchen garden and detached garage on two acres, they discourage me altogether and drive me to my bedroom here on the Upper West Side of Manhattan.

The allure of high-priced real estate and the magical thinking it engenders is rooted in the highly destructive dissatisfaction with one's situation as it really is. Be happy with what you have. Why? Because you actually have it. Do not begrudge Ralph Lauren his hundred-thousand-acre ranch in the Tetons. Nor Mick Jagger his private island in the Bahamas. Nor my friend from college Rick Ratner his mansion in Bedford hunt country, which he inherited from his first wife, whom I suspect he had murdered in a contract killing. Believe me, there are times when each of them envies you. This isn't true, of course, but it's a nice thing to tell yourself.

Envy is one of the most destructive forces in the Universe. Surprisingly, it is rarely the object of the envy that is destroyed by it. Envy can only eat you up from the inside. I should know. I spent much of the last five years as a hollow husk bitterly jealous of the success of radio per-

OH, THE THINGS I KNOW!

sonality Rush Limbaugh. No matter what I did to Rush,
he seemed to get stronger. When I turned off his radio
show in disgust, millions of others turned it on. When I
wrote a book calling him a big fat idiot, he lost weight
and became slightly more accurate.

For every fan who came up to me on the street, ten
dittoheads would curse at me and threaten my kids.
Then, the most crushing blow of all. In July of 2001, as I
struggled to redefine myself in the post-Clinton era, Rush
signed a ten-year contract with radio syndicator Premiere Radio Network for two hundred and fifty million
dollars. More than enough to buy even the most expensive real estate in the back of the *New York Times Magazine*. I was devastated. The cancer of envy was eating
away at my flesh and bones, and worst of all, my soul.

Then one day, in September, my friend Alex Rod-
riguez called me. A-Rod said that he had been listening
to Rush from his thirty-room plantation with formal
gardens and koi pond in the Texas hill country. "Al,"
A-Rod said, "did you hear about Rush? He's deaf!"

You could have knocked me over with a feather. All
that time I had spent envying Rush had been, I realized,
a complete waste of time and psychic energy. I could
have put that time to better use by envying Billy Crystal
or the cast of *Friends*. When I listened to Rush's radio

show the next afternoon, I felt sympathy, even love, for the tubby, right wing gasbag.

To think he could never enjoy the sound of Rage Against the Machine singing their hit song "Bullet in the Head," he could never hear the sound of those firemen booing Hillary Clinton in Madison Square Garden, or even the simple snap, crackle, and pop of that morning's twelfth bowl of Rice Krispies. Rush would miss so much that I took for granted.

There were many who thought that I would be gleeful about Rush's misfortune. Nothing could be further from the truth. In fact, I was among the first to write Rush a personal note expressing my concern not just for his medical condition, but for what seemed to me to be his vulnerable legal situation. You see, when Rush announced that he was deaf, he said that he had started losing his hearing several months previously, in May, which I recall being an exceptionally envious period for myself after Steve Martin did such a good job hosting the Oscars. The problem was Rush had tastefully and considerately kept his condition private, choosing not to burden the representatives of Premiere Radio Network with his personal problems during their negotiations. Unfortunately, from Premiere Radio Network's perspective, they had purchased the services of a Rush Limbaugh in full command of his faculties. It could be said that Rush's deception had been more than just a considerate and tasteful decision on his part, but was instead a form of fraud. The type of fraud which could expose Rush to enormous civil liabilities, or conceivably, in this post-Enron era, even criminal penalties, if the fraud had been undertaken using the mail in any state other than Nevada.

The more I thought about it, the more concerned I became for my old pal Rush. We'd been friends for too many years for me to sit idly by while he was carted off to prison in a large wheelbarrow. I called the lawyers from the Premiere Radio Network and tried to reason with them. I pointed out the consequences of pressing charges against Rush and sending him to prison for even a short, symbolic jail term of, say, five to ten years. Were they aware that the best defense against rape in prison is good hearing? Ironically just the faculty that Rush was now lacking?

To my relief, for the time being anyway, Rush remains a free man, and received a (reportedly successful) cochlear implant on December 18, a Christmas gift not just for Rush and his two pugs, Stinky and Wiggles, but for the Franken family as well.

CHAPTER SUMMARY

Make a list of the things you do have. Then think of all the people who don't have those things. There's no point in making a list of them, since they number in the billions. Then make a list of the things you actually need. Here, I'll make it for you. Food, clothes, shelter. Now, don't you feel like an asshole?

~

CHAPTER 19

Oh, The People You Must Trample to Get Ahead!

Balzac once wrote, "Behind every great fortune is a great crime." While I agree with Balzac (it seems to be true in every case but Oprah's), I part company with him over the question of whether or not this is a good or bad thing. Yes, you must commit crimes to get ahead. So what? You must step on hands, groins, and heads, if necessary, in your own desperate climb to the top of the heap. The sooner you realize this, the sooner you can begin committing the crimes that are necessary to make your way in the world.

Tough talk? Sure. Maybe you like it down there at the bottom with Balzac. Fine. You're no threat to me. Just stay out of my way.

I thought twice before writing this chapter. But then my editor, a vicious, hard-driving rat bastard named Mitch Hoffman, told me that there had to be a chapter where the rubber met the road, where I really let my hair down and told it like it is. Maria Shriver and Anna Quindlen have carefully kept their advice on winning the corporate dogfight to a minimum. Maria merely tells her readers to "go for the jugular" and "not [be] prevented from getting ahead by moral considerations." For Anna, her "get tough" section consists only of a brief anecdote about Genghis Khan, some reluctant commanders, and a cauldron of boiling pitch. That's why their books are worse than worthless. They themselves don't adopt the "take no prisoners" philosophy essential to successful advice book writing.

I'm not going to make the mistake Anna and Maria did, for they are my competitors. Business is warfare, and when I read their books and discovered that they had refrained from attacking each other, I realized that they were weak and cowardly and that their readers were mine for the taking.

It is an invariable law that people rise in life to the extent that they possess the killer instinct and, equally important, the ability to conceal that killer instinct behind a friendly smile. Is this how I got ahead? You're damn right it is! Do you have any idea how many comedians there are who are smarter and more talented than I am who have never made it? Have you ever heard of Rick

Ducommun? He's a genius! But unfortunately for him, he's also a nice guy.

Perhaps you think I shouldn't be telling you all this. That by revealing the truth about my path to the top I am leaving myself vulnerable to aggressive up-and-comers. Nothing could be further from the truth. In fact, by telling you all this, I am playing you like a fiddle. I have you where I want you, dear reader, and now I'm going to crush you.

CHAPTER SUMMARY

In Chapter 5, "Oh, the Drugs You Will Take!" I emphasized the importance of consulting a physician regularly in order to avoid potentially dangerous prescription drug interactions. Or if I didn't, I certainly should have. I wrote this chapter under the influence of the cholesterol-fighting drug Lipitor and a seemingly innocuous over-the-counter nasal spray, Afrin. These, in combination with a vodka and cranberry juice, yielded the results you see above as well as a seven-hour blackout. Now that the nasal spray has worn off, I can assure you that it is not necessary to destroy others in order to advance yourself, and I can justify my ever having said so only in terms of my initial promise to give you bad as well as good advice.

~

CHAPTER 20

Oh, The Books You'll Read!

This isn't the only book you should read. There, I said it. How many other authors would admit that their books were not so utterly comprehensive that they eliminate the need for any other reading? This is, however, the only *advice* book you should read. I know that because in doing the research for this book, I've read all the others and, frankly, they're terrible.

Who is to blame? Not the publishers. They are simply satisfying a demand from the public. No, the fault lies with you, the reader. You are the one who demands quick fixes and comforting clichés. Sure, you're terrific in many ways. So don't beat yourself up about your insatiable appetite for worthless self-help books.

But if I may offer a word of advice, why not spend the time you waste reading self-help books or listening to self-help tapes reading something more worthwhile? For example, biographies. You can learn infinitely more about how to live a meaningful life by reading a biography of someone who did, such as Winston Churchill, than by reading *How to Live a Meaningful Life* by Dr. Leonard and Arlene Shapiro.

For example, by reading a Churchill biography such as *Churchill: A Study in Greatness* by Geoffrey Best, we learn how Churchill conquered his own demons, particularly depression, in order to focus on a more urgent problem at hand, preventing Hitler from conquering Great Britain. Self-help author Dr. Wayne Dyer would describe Churchill's arrogance, obstinacy, and obsessiveness as his "erroneous zones." Yet, in fact, by reading a biography you would learn that it was these very qualities that enabled him to triumph over fascism.

Believe it or not, even a novel, particularly one recommended by Oprah and her popular book club, is less a waste of time than reading a self-help book like the Shapiros' follow-up, *How to Avoid Wasting Time*. Novels can broaden your perspective, take you somewhere in space and time you've never been, and leave you breathless in admiration of the imaginative genius it took to write them. Something you'll never get from reading a book by the Shapiros, even if they wrote a novel.

After biography, the most valuable nonfiction genre is

political satire of the sort practiced by me and Jonathan Swift. A book like *Rush Limbaugh Is a Big Fat Idiot*, by me, can give you a measure of healthy contempt for our so-called leaders while delivering an invigorating quota of endorphin-releasing belly laughs.

Many people believe that reading poetry is good for the soul. Personally, I can't recommend poetry. I don't have time to read anything that's deliberately hard to figure out. If I wanted to read something that didn't make any sense, I'd just read Maria Shriver's book.

There's also no reason to read plays unless you have to for school. See them performed on stage. Or better yet, rent the video or DVD. I know what you're thinking. "Can't I just apply the same principle and watch a biography of Churchill on the History Channel instead of reading a seven-hundred-page book?" No. Plays were meant to be performed or turned into videos. If you want to watch a poetry video, go ahead. I'm not going to stop you. But good luck finding one.

And just don't confine your reading to books. Remember the newspaper. Unlike a book, a newspaper contains up-to-the-minute information like your horoscope and today's "Beetle Bailey." And never forget, just reading the front page of a newspaper can give you a pretty good idea of what's going on in the world. This is the real world, the world that you and I and everyone else lives in. Get to know it. Because it's unlikely you'll ever live in any other.

———

CHAPTER SUMMARY

You're never too old to learn. Unless you have Alzheimer's, in which case you're never too old to unlearn. Either way, continuing education should be a lifelong mission. Many adults choose to return to school after their children have left home. Others pursue a self-directed course of personal improvement through reading biographies, novels, and calculus textbooks. It doesn't matter what you learn, just that you remain committed to learning. Make a solemn pledge to learn at least one new thing a week. This week I'm learning the names of the Great Lakes. Next week I'm learning Italian. But that's next week.

CHAPTER 21

~

Oh, The People You'll Sue!

One of the great pleasures of advancing years is both the threat and the fact of spurious litigation. As you get older, you will find not only that you will want to sue people, but that you will have the time and where-withal to do so. Almost any sort of encounter can generate an entertaining lawsuit. Obviously commercial transactions, whether they be the purchase of a possibly defective product, an unsatisfactory delivery of services, or most importantly, a tenant-landlord relationship, can be a gold mine.

Sometimes, the best way to begin suing people is to sue people close to home, such as a family member. Were you shortchanged by your grandmother's will? Let the court decide. Did your uncle execute it properly? Proba-bly not. There's only one way to find out for sure.

And don't let the stigma and hate mail discourage you

from suing the government in defense of an unpopular cause or principle. Have you ever noticed that every penny produced by the U.S. mint has the words "In God We Trust" stamped on it? That can't be right. Go ahead. Take that one up for me. You might even get the ACLU to pay for it. And how about the fact that the penny has a picture of Abraham Lincoln on it? That's not right either. Somebody should sue. Why not you?

———

CHAPTER SUMMARY

You may remember "al," my Milquetoasty alter ego, as well as "AL!" the self-confident, positive-thinking author of most of this book. You've just met a third of my personalities, "aL." (Note to those who are reading this to the blind. This personality is correctly pronounced "Awwwl.") "aL" combines the paranoia and sense of victimhood that are distinguishing characteristics of "al" with "AL's" arrogant grandiosity. It's not my most productive persona. And I am not saying that just because of what Justice O'Connor wrote in her scathing unanimous decision against me in the case of Franken *v.* U.S. Mint. *Try to resolve your disputes outside of court, through reasonable discussion, a willingness to compromise, or the mediation of a mutually acceptable third party. If that doesn't work, just give up.* **Stay. Out. Of Court!**

Book Three

~

Did you enjoy Book Two? In Book One I covered the immediate postgraduate years. In Book Two we looked at matters familiar to people in their thirties and forties. In Book Three I will cover what cynical advertisers improbably call "the best years of your life." And perhaps if you read this section, they can be, while not the best years of your life, at least better than other people's "best years." But don't wait until the last part of your life to read Book Three. Lessons about the end of your life can help you make intelligent decisions in your earlier years, such as investing in a good catastrophic health care plan.

People who first read this book as it appeared in monthly installments in the Saturday Evening Post said they didn't understand the division into Book One, Book Two, and Book Three. While by necessity there is some arbitrariness in where certain chapters are placed (for instance, you will keep telling yourself stupid things throughout your life), the structure of the book reflects the fact that life is not a steady progression, but falls into distinct phases: youth, middle age, old age, decrepitude, senility, round-the-clock geriatric care, and prolonged agony before death. Originally, I *devoted a separate book to each of these stages. But after my editor read Chapter 91, "Oh, the Vanilla Ensure Is the Only Thing Keeping You Alive!" he encouraged me to focus on Books One through Three and keep Books Four through Seven to be published as a sequel at a later date, perhaps when I myself turn one hundred in the year 2051.*

Here then, Book Three, which will bring you from mid-career to retirement to the final chapter—"Oh, the Nursing Home You'll Wind Up In!"—in order to "ensure" that the book ends on an up note. Enjoy.

CHAPTER 22

~

Oh, the Giving Back to Your Community You Ought to Be Doing Instead of Reading This!

I know that leisure time is precious. Many is the day I would have preferred to have watched a football game, played eighteen holes of golf, or just lain in bed for a couple extra hours of shut-eye instead of giving something back to my community. Many is the day I did.

But on those rare occasions when I have given back something to my community, I've been glad that I did. You see, when you give something back, you also *get* something back in the form of people thinking you're a better person than you actually are. Not only that, you also get back a sense of accomplishment, a warm feeling for your fellow man, and a chance to gain some perspective, such as gratitude for your own circumstances.

"But wait a minute!" you say, "I donate money every year. To the United Way. To my church or synagogue.

111

[See Chapter 9.] To the National Rifle Association. Why should I give my time, too?" Well, the most obvious reason is to undo some of the damage done by your donation to the National Rifle Association. For example, you could volunteer at a hospital that treats a lot of gunshot victims. If that's not your "thang," as the kids say, you could work in a literacy program for underprivileged kids, teaching them not to say things like "thang."

Is there such a thing as giving too much to the community? Yes. Balance in your life is an important theme in this book. For example, take Mother Teresa. While what she did for the poor of Calcutta was commendable, she gave up a number of important things: having a family, exploring sides to her personality other than just the "self-sacrificing living saint" side, and being able to give something back to slightly less hopeless communities like Detroit.

I'm an entertainer. One of the ways I give back is by entertaining. So let me entertain you by giving you an example of how and where I entertain. Recently I returned from my third USO Tour, during which I had the privilege of performing for our men and women in uniform in Germany, Italy, Bosnia, and Kosovo. I wanted to do my part in our effort against the evildoers, and I figured it was either entertain or fight. I know that many of you reading this are just graduating from college and have probably already joined up. Next year instead of playing Hacky Sack in the quad, you'll probably be dodging mortar fire in Iraq or North Korea. I'll be there with you, not carrying a gun or driving a Humvee, but telling jokes and then quickly leaving.

Whenever I entertain the troops, I make an effort to tell crowd-pleasing jokes, not the kind of practical-advice-couched-as-humor that you're enjoying in this book. And yet, as an entertainer, I feel you deserve a little break from the relentlessly cerebral tone I have been taking, which, though entertaining, requires a great deal of concentration and commitment on the part of the reader. Would you like just to be entertained for a little while? Entertained with the very same crowd-pleasing jokes that have been used in USO Tours across the globe? Okay, here goes. But just remember that when I see you next year in Baghdad, I may be doing some of the same material.

I gotta tell ya, *everybody's* caught up in this patriotic fervor, even people I wouldn't expect. After September 11, an old friend of mine went right to his closet and got out his old "America" T-shirt. Of course, it took him four hours to white-out "sucks."

But everybody wants to do their part. My same friend told me he's going to stop buying heroin. Hit the Taliban in the pocketbook.

You know, our military and the Taliban's are very different. Though we do have one thing in common. Neither side allows women in combat. Though the Taliban take it a step further. They don't allow women to go outside. Or to hum. Or to look up.

I'll tell ya, one thing Afghanistan proved. Bombing works! Not that there are a lot of targets there. In fact, so far we've flown over forty-three hundred sorties, dropped over seven hundred tons of ordnance, and done just thirty-seven dollars in damage. But we're a compassionate nation. After this is all over, we're going to put the dirt and rocks back where they were before this thing started.

You know, President Bush says this is a different type of war, in which we have to use every tool at our disposal: military, diplomacy, intelligence, financial, law enforcement. Here's a tool I'd like to keep on the table: Torture. I mean we have like nine hundred detainees. I'm not talking about all of them. I mean the guy who's got an apartment in Paterson, New Jersey, but was inquiring about crop dusting. That guy knows something. Now, we know he's willing to die for his cause. But is he willing to take a hot red poker up the ass? That's what I want to know. Now, we know he wants to service those seventy-two black-eyed virgins in Paradise. Does he think he can do that after we've crushed his balls?

Now, just because you can't tell great jokes like these in front of cheering crowds of thousands, that doesn't mean you can't give something back yourself. What are you good at? Are you good at serving people in a soup line? Then do that. Most people without specialized skills can at least learn to ladle.

Can you read? If you've gotten this far in the book, it's safe to say you probably can. Consider reading to the blind. The blind enjoy the same kind of books you and I do. Mysteries, biographies, and especially advice books. Read this book to the blind, and I can guarantee you that when you get to this part, you'll be rewarded with a smile that will be worth every minute you spent on the bus getting to the blind person's house. Right, blind person?

"But, Al, I'm a brain surgeon. Ladling soup or reading to the blind would take valuable time away from the life-saving operations I perform." That's no excuse. As I said earlier, the point in giving back is not actually what you give, but what you receive. And I think you, Mr. Arrogant Brain Surgeon, need more than anyone to learn the valuable lesson you will receive by reading the newest Jackie Collins novel to a blind senior.

Besides brain surgeons, another group of people who often make excuses for not giving back to their communities are parents. "But I don't have enough time to give to my own kids, much less someone else's," they might say. Well, numbnuts, have you ever thought of giving something back *with* your children? Little kids love homeless outreach programs. To them the homeless are not dirty and scary. They are not smelly. Seeing a homeless person through the eyes of a child can be an experience you'll never forget.

My own personal breakthrough with the homeless came when my daughter decided to bring a sandwich to a homeless man I'll call Earl. My wife puzzled for hours over what sort of sandwich to make for Earl. Would he like a turkey sandwich? A BLT? Or perhaps chicken salad on a kaiser roll? After watching my wife make repeated false starts, my daughter suggested, "Hey, Mom, why don't we just *ask* Earl what kind of sandwich he wants?" This simple solution had never occurred to my wife and me because we were not seeing Earl as a person, but rather as a thing. My daughter and I went out and found Earl at the Chase branch around the corner, opening the door for unappreciative customers at the ATM.

"What kind of sandwiches do you like, Mr. Earl?" my daughter asked, forgetting that Earl was just what we called him and probably not his actual name. Earl quickly explained that instead of a sandwich, he would prefer some money to buy a bottle of muscatel. This, in turn, inspired a healthy and somewhat overdue family discussion on the dangers of alcohol abuse. The Frankens learned a lesson. And Earl got his muscatel!

═══════

CHAPTER SUMMARY

Whatever you give, you get back tenfold. Not literally, say in the form of ten bottles of muscatel. But figuratively, in the form of riches that are truly priceless. For example, when you donate your used car or truck to a charitable organization, you can deduct the full blue book value even if that is many times more than anyone would pay you in cash for it.

CHAPTER 23

~

Oh, Watch Out for Disgruntled Former Employees!

Congratulations! You've made it to the top! Through talent, hard work, and wiliness, tempered with ordinary human decency. You are now the boss. Sit back, take a deep breath, enjoy it. But don't get too comfortable. For every dozen young bucks out there who are gunning for you in a figurative sense, there may be one or two who are quite literally gunning for you . . . with a gun.

One of the most common pitfalls of reaching the pinnacle of success is being shot and killed by a disgruntled former employee. Which is why gathering tips culled from law enforcement experts, security professionals, and dying shooting victims has become something of a personal crusade of mine.

To make amends for the bad advice I gave you in chapter 1, I would like to share with you the fruits of my

118

research in the form of advice that, in a very real sense, might save your life. You may think that the best way to eliminate the problem of disgruntled former employees is never to fire anyone and, indeed, to promote all of your employees regularly, regardless of their abilities or accomplishments. This may work for some businesses, such as Starbucks, but believe me, it does not work for most of them. You won't be the boss for long if you don't occasionally thin out the deadwood.

As we learn every six weeks or so, this process is not without its hazards. Ideally, you will have identified high-risk (to you) employees long before the inevitable necessity of firing them arrives. That way you will know when to start wearing your bulletproof vest. I hope that Harvey Mackay, author of *Swim with the Sharks Without Being Eaten Alive,* will forgive me for cribbing a little bit from his best-selling advice book. In chapter 97, "How to Spot a Future Disgruntled Former Employee," Mackay suggests that you start a Nazi regalia collectors club at your place of work and see who turns up. Or alternatively host a "Bring Your Own Firearm" target-shooting picnic. See who brings guns, how many guns, what kind of guns they bring, and how good they are at shooting the targets.

Now you know who to watch out for. Ironically, they

will almost invariably be the people you should have fired long ago. The only problem is once you begin firing them, they will begin firing at you. Here's a list that you should cut out and keep in a wallet next to my list on world religions from best to worst.

PLACES TO HIDE
ONCE THE SHOOTING STARTS

1. Under the desk

2. In the closet

3. In the closet behind some coats

4. Behind your secretary or coworker

5. In that little room where they keep the phone-switching equipment

6. In the parking lot, behind a car

7.

8.

9.

10.

I have left the last four blank for you to fill in based on the specific layout of your workplace. For example, if you work in a tannery, you may want to hide in one of the barrels in which they keep the rotting animal offal. The killer is not likely to look for you there.

This is more than just a model of how to avoid being shot on the job. It is a paradigm for being an effective boss in general. Take proactive steps to get to know your employees better. Know their strengths, sure. But also know their weaknesses and their mental illnesses. Know the layout of your workplace. It will be as effective in helping you speedily usher a client to your office as it will be in avoiding a rampaging killer.

Chapter Summary

Harvey Mackay tells a funny story about the first meeting of the Nazi Regalia Collectors Club at the Mackay Envelope Company in Minneapolis. After calling the meeting to order, Harvey went around the room asking the participants what sort of Nazi regalia they were most interested in. Pretty much everyone said the Luger, except a small quiet man in the corner who expressed an interest in Nazi footwear and medals from Rommel's Afrika Korps. Feeling it was safe to do so, Harvey fired him immediately. But before even a week had passed, the man returned to the Mackay Envelope Company dressed as a storm trooper and firebombed Harvey's Cadillac.

CHAPTER 24

~

Oh, The Places You'll Call!

If I could summarize my goal in writing this book in a single sentence, it would be this: I want to write a book that will change the life of everyone who reads it for the better. But that isn't a realistic goal. That's just another suffering invitation. A more realistic goal would be that it will change the lives of some people for the better, and it remains my hope that it may do that. Still, it seems prudent to establish a goal that I know for a fact I can accomplish. In this case, to provide *some* information that at least *some* people will find useful at *some* time in their lives.

Almost everyone at some point will make a phone call to a foreign country. If you have, you know how time-consuming and frustrating it can be to find the correct country code for the place you are dialing. No longer. After painstaking research, I have compiled a list of over two hundred and fifty country codes which should satisfy the needs of all but the most prolific overseas callers. This list has it all—from Afghanistan to Zimbabwe—and includes such rarely called places as Antarctica, Gabon, and Portugal. While it would be an exaggeration to say that people have died preparing this list, it is no exaggeration to say that just knowing that it is possible to call the French Antilles, Azerbaijan, or Easter Island will bring joy to the hearts of millions. If anyone asks you if Al Franken's *Oh, the Things I Know!* is worth $10.00, you tell them that the international dialing code list is worth $10.00 all by itself. You'll notice that for added ease of use I've put the list in alphabetical order.

Country Name	Country Code	Country Name	Country Code
Afghanistan	93	Cook Islands	682
Albania	355	Costa Rica	506
Algeria	213	Croatia	385
American Samoa	684	Cuba	53
Andorra	376	Cuba (Guantánamo Bay)	5399
Angola	244	Curaçao	599
Anguilla	264	Cyprus	357
Antarctica	672	Czech Republic	420
Antigua	268	Denmark	45
Argentina	54	Diego Garcia	246
Armenia	374	Djibouti	253
Aruba	297	Dominica	767
Ascension Island	247	Dominican Republic	809
Australia	61	East Timor	670
Austria	43	Easter Island	56
Azerbaijan	994	Ecuador	593
Bahamas	242	Egypt	20
Bahrain	973	El Salvador	503
Bangladesh	880	Equatorial Guinea	240
Barbados	246	Eritrea	291
Barbuda	268	Estonia	372
Belarus	375	Ethiopia	251
Belgium	32	Faeroe Islands	298
Belize	501	Falkland Islands	500
Benin	229	Fiji Islands	679
Bermuda	441	Finland	358
Bhutan	975	France	33
Bolivia	591	French Antilles	596
Bosnia and Herzegovina	387	French Guiana	594
Botswana	267	French Polynesia	689
Brazil	55	Gabon	241
British Virgin Islands	284	Gambia	220
Brunei	673	Georgia	995
Bulgaria	359	Germany	49
Burkina Faso	226	Ghana	233
Burundi	257	Gibraltar	350
Cambodia	855	Greece	30
Cameroon	237	Greenland	299
Canada	1	Grenada	473
Cape Verde Islands	238	Guadeloupe	590
Cayman Islands	345	Guam	671
Central African Republic	236	Guantánamo Bay	5399
Chad	235	Guatemala	502
Chatham Island (New Zealand)	64	Guinea (PRP)	224
Chile	56	Guinea-Bissau	245
China (PRC)	86	Guyana	592
Christmas Island	61	Haiti	509
Cocos-Keeling Islands	61	Honduras	504
Colombia	57	Hong Kong	852
Comoros	269	Hungary	36
Congo	242	Iceland	354
Congo, Dem. Rep. of (former Zaire)	243	India	91

Indonesia	62	New Caledonia	687
Iran	98	New Zealand	64
Iraq	964	Nicaragua	505
Ireland	353	Niger	227
Israel	972	Nigeria	234
Italy	39	Niue	683
Ivory Coast (Côte d'Ivoire)	225	Norfolk Island	672
Jamaica	876	Northern Mariana Islands	
Japan	81	(Saipan, Rota, and Tinian)	670
Jordan	962	Norway	47
Kazakhstan	7	Oman	968
Kenya	254	Pakistan	92
Kirgiz Republic	996	Palau	680
Kiribati	686	Palestine	970
Korea (North)	850	Panama	507
Korea (South)	82	Papua New Guinea	675
Kuwait	965	Paraguay	595
Laos	856	Peru	51
Latvia	371	Philippines	63
Lebanon	961	Poland	48
Lesotho	266	Portugal	351
Liberia	231	Puerto Rico	787
Libya	218	Qatar	974
Liechtenstein	423	Réunion Island	262
Lithuania	370	Romania	40
Luxembourg	352	Russia	7
Macau	853	Rwanda	250
Macedonia (former Yugoslav Rep.)	389	St. Helena	290
Madagascar	261	St. Kitts/Nevis	869
Malawi	265	St. Lucia	758
Malaysia	60	St. Pierre and Miquelon	508
Maldives	960	St. Vincent and Grenadines	784
Mali Republic	223	San Marino	378
Malta	356	São Tomé and Principe	239
Marshall Islands	692	Saudi Arabia	966
Martinique	596	Senegal	221
Mauritania	222	Serbia	381
Mauritius	230	Seychelles Islands	248
Mayotte Island	269	Sierra Leone	232
Mexico	52	Singapore	65
Micronesia (Federated States of)	691	Slovak Republic	421
Midway Island	808	Slovenia	386
Moldova	373	Solomon Islands	677
Monaco	377	Somalia	252
Mongolia	976	South Africa	27
Montserrat	664	Spain	34
Morocco	212	Sri Lanka	94
Mozambique	258	Sudan	249
Myanmar	95	Suriname	597
Namibia	264	Swaziland	268
Nauru	674	Sweden	46
Nepal	977	Switzerland	41
Netherlands	31	Syria	963
Netherlands Antilles	599	Taiwan	886
Nevis	869	Tajikistan	992

Tanzania	255	U.S. Virgin Islands	340	
Thailand	66	Uruguay	598	
Togo	228	Uzbekistan	998	
Tokelau Islands	690	Vanuatu	678	
Tonga Islands	676	Vatican City	39	
Trinidad and Tobago	868	Venezuela	58	
Tunisia	216	Vietnam	84	
Turkey	90	Wake Island	808	
Turkmenistan	993	Wallis and Futuna Islands	681	
Turks and Caicos Islands	649	Western Samoa	685	
Tuvalu	688	Yemen	967	
Uganda	256	Yugoslavia	381	
Ukraine	380	Zambia	260	
United Arab Emirates	971	Zanzibar	255	
United Kingdom	44	Zimbabwe	263	
United States of America	1			

Use this space to jot down your most frequently used country codes!

My Most Frequently Used Country Codes

Country   *Code*   *Who in the country I like to talk to*

1. _____

2. _____

3. _____

4. _____

5. _____

6. _____

CHAPTER SUMMARY

For routine overseas communication it probably makes more sense to use e-mail than the telephone. It's far less expensive and there's less chance that you wake someone in the middle of the night. If, for example, you're confirming a hotel reservation in Paris, there's no reason to call. An e-mail message is sufficient. If on the other hand you want to convey condolences to a friend in Nepal for the assassination of his country's royal family, a phone call has a more personal touch.

CHAPTER 25

~

Oh, The Best Is Yet to Come!

I believe I began the book by telling you about my father. I'm pretty sure that's what I did, but I'm trying to finish now and don't have time to check. As I watched my father age and deteriorate, progressively losing his hearing and his car keys, it used to bother me that these signs of impending mortality didn't bother him more. How could he be so calm and happy, I wanted to know, when it seemed like he had so little to look forward to?

I now believe that my dad had realized a timeless truth. That despite infirmities that begin to manifest themselves as we age, as we get older, life becomes easier. Gone is the lust for fame and vainglory that drives us to rise from junior associate to senior associate. Gone, the fruitless quest for unattainable sexual partners like movie stars such as Halle Berry or movie stars that have been dead for decades, like Marilyn Monroe. Gone, the petty jealousies and frustrations which come from keeping up with the Joneses, or in my case, keeping up with my next-door neighbor, violin virtuoso Yitzhak Perlman. Gone, the kids. Gone, their friends.

For many people, the golden years from fifty to a hundred and twenty are the first time in their lives when they are truly free. Your nest isn't empty, it's full—of possibilities. Whether you choose to travel the world on an ocean liner or travel your neighborhood on one of those electric scooters, the world is your oyster. A wheelchair-accessible oyster!

In the youth of old age, the early fifties, your daily routine will probably be unchanged from what it was during the old age of youth, your late forties. These are your peak earning years, so you're likely to still be working. Though perhaps you will have started to coast a bit.

As your fifties progress, you will run out of momentum and will no longer be able even to coast. You will become "deadwood," the absolute apex of the American corporate pyramid. In his best-seller *Jack: Straight from the Gut,* the legendary G.E. chairman Jack Welch writes with great affection about his fifteen years as the deadwood atop G.E.'s corporate heap. "I'd pull a decision or two out of my ass every month or so on the golf course," Jack writes. "And for that they paid me millions!" That's winning the Jack Welch way.

While you might not qualify for the Deadwood Hall of Fame, like Jack Welch or Secretary of State Colin Powell, in most modern American corporations, you can still overstay your welcome by a good half dozen years. When you are eventually forced into retirement, consider your options. In some businesses you may get a bigger settlement if you go kicking and screaming. In others, simply threatening to kick and scream may be enough to earn you an undeservedly generous retirement package.

While the track outlined above may be the norm, there are plenty of people who have to add "getting hosed at the end of their work life" to the list of things they no longer care about in their golden years. Enron employees come to mind. Also, many self-employed people fail to plan properly for their retirement and wind up having to work well into their hundreds, such as the *60 Minutes* cast.

The fact that Mike Wallace, Morley Safer, and Andy Rooney are still alive underlines the importance of remaining active—and inquisitive—in your declining years. Your children, now adults, will now be having children of their own. Or, if they're gay or infertile, they'll soon be adopting Chinese orphans. Grandparenthood offers the chance to repeat the mistakes of parenthood but with less life-scarring impact on either party. Go ahead, belittle their accomplishments, the way you did with your own kids. Their parents will simply tell them to ignore you.

The years of semiretirement and retirement are a time to explore yourself and find out what you're really interested in. The Civil War was an interesting period. Are you interested in that? No? What about fly-fishing? No? How about exploring your genealogy? No? A vegetable garden! That would be fun! No? You know what's really interesting? Fine cabinetmaking! No? Okay, that was a long shot. You used to enjoy knitting. Why don't you try picking that up again? No? I'll bet some guys from your old Army unit have some interesting hobbies. How about looking them up? No? Jesus Christ! You're just like every other old person I know.

Well, fine! Just sit there.

CHAPTER SUMMARY

Remember earlier in the book I talked about the responsibility of the person receiving the advice, e.g., you the reader? I was really starting to feel at the end of this last chapter that you weren't doing your part. Every suggestion I made, and there were many good ones, got shot down. I don't think you're really pulling your weight. If you don't think you can improve your attitude, why don't you do us both a favor and stop reading right here.

~

CHAPTER 26

Oh, What Doesn't Kill You Can Have Lingering Aftereffects!

A wise man once said to me, "What doesn't kill you will make you stronger." A week later he went in for back surgery, which actually went well and did make him stronger, at least for the time being. However, the blood clot that formed in his leg during surgery, although it didn't kill him, caused a pulmonary embolism, collapsing his left lung. He will never regain full capacity of that lung, and instead of stronger, he is markedly weaker and wheezes like a freight train.

Once again, let's take a look at the scientific literature. Scientists tell us that, as you age, you will become fatter, weaker, and more disgusting. There is a reason, for example, why adult-onset diabetes is not called simply "diabetes." It's because it "sets on" you when you are an adult, usually because you have become grossly overweight.

Most diseases that will afflict you as you age, however, are beyond your control. Bacteria and viruses are all around you. They are in the air you breathe, the food you eat, and the gay men you have sex with. There's nothing you can do about it.

Scientists tell us that human beings were not intended to live past forty. Advances in medicine and nutrition have prolonged our lives long past our physical peak, which usually occurs when we are about thirteen. In the ninety years we often live past our prime, we will steadily deteriorate until we are able to do little more than grin toothlessly for the video camera and claim that the secret to our long life is the glass of red wine we have every day.

(A brief digression on whether that suspicious-looking mole is actually cancer. Even without looking at it, I can tell you that it probably is. Take this simple test called the ABC test. "A" is for age. What is your age? Is it over thirteen? If so, it's cancer. That's how the ABC test works.)

For men, a prime indicator, the canary in the coal mine if you will, of your overall health is the prostate, the troublesome walnut-sized gland that sits proudly between your balls and your asshole. An enlarged prostate won't kill you and it can make you stronger—if you feel stronger because of the exercise you get walking to and from the bathroom seventeen times a night to pass a few drops of urine. You may even feel stronger if you have to sit down to pee in the middle of the night because your back is bothering you. But I doubt it. Instead you will probably feel less than 100 percent virile. And to think, you just turned thirty!

While women are not in on the fun of the prostate and its many moods, they do have many special physical conditions that men cannot enjoy. Such as ectopic pregnancies; endometriosis, which has something to do with the lining of the uterus; and the granddaddy, or should I say, grandmommy of them all, menopause. Many funny one-woman shows have been done about menopause, although I personally am waiting for Paula Poundstone's. But rarely do we get the man's perspective on this female problem.

There you have it. By calling menopause a "problem," I am characterizing it in a masculine way as a negative thing rather than something that is beautiful, and womanly, and life-affirming. That's because I'm speaking from personal experience. Because while my wife may have felt more womanly while going through menopause, she certainly acted more "bitchily." So, that's what I'm going on.

As a practical matter, the list of maladies, diseases, and conditions you may suffer from during your life is literally infinite. Yet, in keeping with my desire that this book be practical as well as inspiring, I have prepared a much shorter list, which you can also clip out and save, of common medical problems associated with aging and the things that you love that cause them.

Thing You Love	What It Causes
Bacon	Arteriosclerosis
Marlboro Lights	Lung Cancer
Dunkin' Donuts	Diabetes/colon cancer
Johnnie Walker Black	Cirrhosis
Johnnie Walker Red	Pancreatitis
Jessica from the office	Herpes
Steven the bartender	Anal Warts
Not wearing a seatbelt	Impact Trauma
Starbucks triple shot latte	Heart arrhythmia
The Bold and the Beautiful	Obesity/adult-onset diabetes
Travel to exotic places	Hepatitis B
Travel to Florida	Skin Cancer
An exciting new job	Irritable Bowel Syndrome
Skiing	Sonny Bono Syndrome

The good news, and there is some good news, is that many of the physical complaints that we suffer from because we live so much longer than we're supposed to can be treated and sometimes cured thanks to advances in technology similar to those which have served to keep us alive so long. I'm speaking, of course, of baldness, which can be kind of cured by Minoxidil.

―――――

CHAPTER SUMMARY

As you get older, you will almost certainly get sicker. But rather than seeing your ailments as afflictions, see them as badges of merit in the scouting expedition that is life. Liver spots, gouty toes, and chronic flatulence may not be beautiful in the classic sense, but they are the distinguishing characteristics that brand you as a survivor and deserving of every bit of the respect accorded to senior citizens in our society.

CHAPTER 27

~

Oh, Laughter Is the Best Medicine!

As a professional comedian, I can't tell you what a relief it is to come to a chapter topic on which I have some actual expertise. Undoubtably you have heard the expression "Laughter is the best medicine" before, and I can tell you for a fact that it isn't. Medicine is the best medicine.

Let's say you were suffering from a severe case of flesh-eating bacteria. Would you rather be treated by a doctor who would prescribe an antibiotic? Or by comedian Chris Rock, who would tell you how flesh-eating bacteria was not a problem in his neighborhood, because the bacteria were afraid of the tough motherfuckers who lived there? Funny? Indubitably. But believe me, when your lungs are turning into bloody foam, the last thing you want to do is start laughing.

While clearly not the best medicine, laughter, along

with chuckling, chortling, guffawing, and even the extremely mild form of amusement you are experiencing right now, has a palliative effect on your psyche. The relationship between mind and body (see Chapter 77, "Oh, Putting the Placebo Effect to Work for You!") has been firmly established in the scientific literature as the key to understanding the healing process.

In its simplest form the relationship can be illustrated this way: Good Mind = Good Body; Bad Mind = Bad Body. And what is more indicative of a good mind than a good sense of humor? A quality which, by the way, many *Playboy* Playmates claim is a turn-on, along with wearing a pukka shell necklace. If any man could ever successfully combine the two—and I've never seen it done—he could turn on any Playmate he met.

The effect of laughter is more than just psychological. When you laugh, your body releases endorphins, and every so often, if you laugh really hard, a small amount of diarrhea. Like a good orgasm or a good sneeze, a good laugh relieves unhealthy pent-up tensions which can cause an imbalance in the body's humors—specifically an excess of black bile—which we have known since the Middle Ages is the cause of all illness.

Beyond its clearly established physiological powers, laughing is just plain fun. Try to laugh once a day. Read this book until you laugh. Then put it down. You've laughed enough for today. Pick it up tomorrow. Continue reading, slowly and carefully to make sure you don't miss anything funny. Did you laugh? Then put the book down. For some, this book will provide a laugh a day for many years. For others, you may have to reread the book many times before you laugh even once. Don't give up. The laughs are here. You just have to find them.

CHAPTER SUMMARY

Have you heard the one about the guy who goes to the doctor with a dot on his forehead? The doctor says, "Oh my God! I've never seen this before, but I read about it in medical school. In six weeks you're going to have a full-sized penis growing out of your forehead." "Well, cut it out!" says the patient. "I can't," says the doctor. "It's attached to your brain—you'd die." "Oh my God!" says the patient. "So you're saying that in six weeks every morning when I wake up and look in the mirror, I'm going to see a penis growing out of my forehead?" "Oh, you won't see it," says the doctor. "The balls will cover your eyes." *

---

*That classic joke was first told to me on an airplane by Buddy Hackett, the comedian who made my dad cough up phlegm.

143

CHAPTER 28

~

Oh, The Loneliness,
The Loneliness!

During the brief time we spend here on earth, each one of us will confront the same unanswerable question. What is the meaning of life? Some may find a facile and semi-satisfying answer in religion, especially if they choose one of the higher-ranked religions on my list in Chapter 9. For others solace will come from the handy oblivion offered by a bottle of bourbon, a hypodermic needle, or meaningless sex with an endless number of faceless partners.

But most of us, surrounded as we are by omnipresent reminders of the hopelessness and futility of the human condition, will not be able to take lasting comfort in any of these, even the sex.

The tragic fact is that we are born alone and we die alone, even though in both cases, we may be surrounded by family, friends, family friends, doctors and nurses, some of whom might be family friends. In the same way, though we may spend our whole lives surrounded by others, many of whom may be very dear to us, we are always just one step away from a bottomless chasm called loneliness, into which we may plunge at any moment.

How many times have you stood in the center of a glamorous party peopled with movie stars, famous artists, and persons of note in the worlds of business and politics, all of them there to celebrate the publication of your latest book? You are the center of attention. Everyone wants to talk to you, to hear your opinions or tell you the latest joke. And yet you feel strangely disassociated. You have to fight an urge to flee, to find a refuge where you can be as physically isolated as you feel spiritually and emotionally.

But you can't flee. They'd all catch on and realize what kind of pathetic fraud you actually are. You are trapped. So you excuse yourself and escape to the host's bedroom, where you jerk off into Dominick Dunne's hat. Yes, it's comforting for the time being. And you may even manage a smile when you hear the hostess apologize to Dunne and blame the dog a few minutes later. But such joys are fleeting and very soon despair returns.

The Latin poet Horace once wrote, "Life is a comedy to those who think and a tragedy to those who feel." To which I like to add, "And vice versa." So what is to be done? How are we to escape from the perilous maze of existence?

The answer is love. And not just of self. Or hat. But the type of love in which one's being is merged with that of another. The type of love through which we glimpse, albeit fleetingly, the depths of another's soul and they glimpse ours. I've never experienced this type of love. Perhaps that's why people think I'm cynical. But I remain ever hopeful, and that's why I say in addition to love the answer is also hope.

Yes, hope. The hope that the dawn of each new day heralds an infinite number of undreamt of opportunities. Every one of which will be mine when I wake up in about three or four hours.

There you have it. Life's meaning can be found in hopeful expectancy of absolute and unconditional love. Look around you. The Korean man behind the counter in the deli. The old woman carrying her shopping bags. The student. The businessman. Anna Quindlen. Maria Shriver. Ben Franklin. All of them ever hopeful, believing in the eternal possibility of a merging of souls with their fellow man.

Okay, I may have gotten carried away. I honestly don't know why most people bother to get up in the morning, and I often think things might be better if they didn't.

CHAPTER SUMMARY

HALT! Don't write when you're hungry, angry, lonely, or tired. H.A.L.T. Since finishing this last chapter, I've taken a nap, eaten a granola bar, spent some time with my black lab Kirby, and as a result feel a lot less angry. So who knows what the meaning of life is? And who cares? Have fun. How? Read the next chapter!

CHAPTER 29

~

Oh, The Nursing Home You'll Wind Up In!

As we approach the end of this book, it is entirely appropriate that we discuss the final fifty years of life, which, if the scientific literature is to be believed, will take many of us from age one hundred to one hundred and fifty. Yes, that's right. By the time most recent college graduates are old, advances in medicine will have extended the human life span to almost a century and a half.

You can expect the first fifty years of your life to be good. The second fifty will be not so good. The last fifty years will be absolutely horrible. That's what the experts say.

However long you live, unless you are lucky enough to die in an accident or by suicide, you are probably going to spend your last years in a nursing home, or as I prefer to call it, an assisted-care senior living community. That sounds better, doesn't it?

No matter what you call it, it's not something most people look forward to. But let me tell you, a great deal of this apprehension is the result of ignorance, pure and simple. Do yourself a favor. Visit a nursing home. Tell them you have a senile aunt you're thinking of having committed against her will. You'll get the grand tour, believe you me.

Sure, you're going to see a lot of very old people in their pajamas, sitting in their wheelchairs, nodding or simply staring into space. Yes, you may smell stale urine or hear the loud incoherent ravings of "residents" who don't want to take their meds. But that's not the whole picture. Many nursing homes have swimming pools, where sprightly seniors can enjoy life-prolonging aerobic exercise. Some have dance classes or daily Bible study. Sometimes romance can blossom in a nursing home. Between a female nurse and the wealthiest and sickest of the male residents. Or between a male nurse and a male dance instructor.

Yes, life goes on in the nursing home, although it goes on much more pleasantly in some nursing homes than in others. At the risk of sounding like a broken record, the key to getting the most out of your nursing home experience is a positive attitude. Try to view your stay as merely temporary, because, in one way or another, it is. Get a TV in your room and watch positive television programs such as *Touched by an Angel*. Don't be afraid to follow the example set by the feisty seniors you'll see on your television, especially in bad comedies. It won't be long before you're "boogy, oogy, oogying" to the latest hip-hop smash hit and getting your freak on with a partner seven-eighths your age.

I would be remiss if I did not conclude this book with a few words about the very end of life, which, in case you hadn't noticed, is death. Like graduation from college, death is not an ending, it is a beginning, a commencement, if you will. The commencement of a journey and an adventure for which no book can prepare you. Although I do not know what awaits us past the gates of death, I do know this: Your "cemetery years" will be a lot more satisfying and productive if you approach them with a positive attitude.

═══════

CHAPTER SUMMARY

For both nursing homes and cemeteries an educated consumer is the best customer. Remember, you'll be an eternity in one and what seems like an eternity in the other.

Oh, the Afterword!

Having just dictated the final chapter, I am left with that special sense of vertigo one gets when contemplating eternity. Eternity, an infinite amount of time, is difficult for many people to comprehend. Even half of an eternity is hard to get a handle on. Our lives are an almost infinitesimal moment in the vast sweep of time. And yet, to us, our lives and what we accomplish during them are very important. They stand as our monument—perhaps for all eternity.

What would you have people say of you three hundred million years in the future? Undoubtedly you'd want them to say that you were a good parent. And that you cultivated several life-enriching hobbies. And you probably wouldn't even mind if they pointed out that you'd faked a couple of orgasms on occasion. As I imagine those future students of the life and times of

Al Franken, I like to think of them reading this book, perhaps in pill form. Not because I'm proud of every word, far from it. But because it will have meaning for their lives. Yes, things will be different three million centuries hence. Their drugs will have different names; there may be five sexes instead of two, and advances in science may have eliminated real estate envy altogether. But while some of the specifics may have changed, I am positive my core message will be as relevant, if not *more* relevant, than it is today.

Sure, there will still be the need for the personal note. Yes, your spouse's face will still make your skin crawl. And while your children may be grown in vats instead of a mother's womb, they will still watch violent television or perhaps violent 3-D smell-o-vision.

But beyond the petty details of life on Earth and maybe Venus, my answer to the all-important question "why are we here?" will still be true in the year 300,002,002 A.D. What is that answer? I think I touched on it in either chapter seven or twenty-six. And that's really the point, isn't it? We must each find our own answers, either by looking back at chapter seven or twenty-six, or by living each day to the fullest, or, short of that, catching up on your rest so that you can get the most out of tomorrow or the day after that if you're really exhausted.

So, that's it. We're done. We have journeyed together from the limitless promise of college graduation, through repeated failures, all the way to the nursing home. When we set out, I made it clear that as advisor and advisee we each have responsibilities and share equally in the burden of advice-giving. I think it's fair to say that I have more than held up my end of the bargain. Have you done your part? Only time will tell. But that thing you did yesterday was a good start!

Oh, the Acknowledgments!

~

Huge gratitude to my editor, Mitch Hoffman, who was the first to suggest that I apologize to my wife in these acknowledgments. His terrific and very supportive number two, Stephanie Bowe, who concurred. Carole Baron, my publisher, who offered me more money if I'd make fun of my wife, and encouraged me to use the extra money to buy her something nice. To my kids—I'm sorry I broke my promise not to write anything that could upset Mom. Jonathon Lazear, my literary agent, who personally called my wife to help smooth things over. My assistant, Liz Topp, who dutifully hid the material from my wife during the writing process. Good job, Liz! My attorney, Gunnar Erickson (and by the way—all those people who said I was crazy not to have a Jew lawyer, they're wrong), who assured me that what I wrote is not grounds for divorce as long as I apologize in

155

these acknowledgments. Dutton's graphic design and publicity teams refrained from expressing an opinion about my wife, which I think was appropriate given the amount of time we actually spent together.

Which brings me to my wife, Franni. Honey, there's no need for you to read this book. Why? Because you're perfect already. And everything I've learned about being a good person and living a good life comes from you. If people come up to you and tell you that, for example, there is a chapter titled "Oh, Just Looking at Your Spouse Will Make Your Skin Crawl!" remember that in my writing I often create hypothetical "what if" situations, and that chapter was a prime example. But to the extent those hypothetical "what if" characterizations of the imaginary composite spouse referred to in the book has caused you any discomfort, I apologize. Throughout our thirty-two years together you've always been supportive and you've always laughed at my jokes, good and bad. Thank you for giving me the freedom to make them all, and for being a good sport. I know if our places were reversed, I'd be really, really mad. I love you.

Now that that's out of the way, I really must acknowledge Oprah, who has done so much for the publishing industry. As I write these acknowledgments, I have no idea whether *Oh, the Things I Know!* will be an Oprah

Book Club Selection. If it is, believe me, I'll be thrilled. Thank you, Oprah. You're *a class act*.

Finally, I am often asked about my influences as a comedian and a writer, and, while I usually cite some revered names like Jack Benny and Bob and Ray, I want to avail myself of this opportunity to acknowledge a less well-known humorist—Billy Kimball. As I wrote this book, there was not a moment when I did not feel Billy's presence. Thank you, Billy. Wherever you are.

Oh, About the Typeface!

This book is printed in Sabon. Sabon was, admittedly, not my first choice for the type in this book. I wanted something more upscale like Geneva or, maybe, Times Roman. But they weren't available so I decided to go with Sabon. I think you'll agree that, while not great, it's a perfectly good, readable typeface.